BIRDS
FROM BRICKS

Amazing LEGO® Designs That Take Flight

Thomas Poulsom

QUARRY

Quarto is the authority on a wide range of topics.

Quarto educates, entertains and enriches the lives of our readers—enthusiasts and lovers of hands-on living.

www.QuartoKnows.com

First published in the United States of America in 2016 by
Quarry Books, an imprint of
Quarto Publishing Group USA Inc.
100 Cummings Center
Suite 406-L
Beverly, Massachusetts 01915-6101
Telephone: (978) 282-9590
Fax: (978) 283-2742
QuartoKnows.com
Visit our blogs at QuartoKnows.com

10 9 8 7 6 5 4 3 2 1

ISBN: 978-1-63159-079-5

Digital edition published in 2016
eISBN: 978-1-62788-841-7

Library of Congress Cataloging-in-Publication Data is available.

Design: Traffic Design Consultants
Page Layout: Sporto
Photography: Landun Reimer and Austin Granger; Shutterstock, pages 142 and 143; Getty, kakapo image on page 143
Illustration: Daniel Siskind, Erik Knopp, and Yitzy Kasowitz

Printed in China

PREFACE

After getting back into my childhood passion of LEGO building and combining that with my love of nature, I decided to experiment with creating other LEGO bird designs and was met with overwhelming interest. My official set of three LEGO birds was simply not enough for my fellow bird and LEGO enthusiasts. The LEGO project that started with Bobby the Robin Red Breast has now expanded into more than eighty different birds; I've included fifteen in this book for your LEGO-building pleasure. The birds featured hail from each continent on Earth, incorporating my favorite species from every corner of the world.

Because of their diversity, I've included detailed information about each individual bird to feed your curiosity. You'll find out how they nest, what they eat, their flocking patterns, and much more. Learning more about each bird will help you during the step-by-step building process, which I've also included in-depth instructions for.

Crafted with entirely factual accuracy, this new set of birds is perfect for children, adults with a LEGO-building passion, and bird lovers alike. Each bird you create will look realistic and simply elegant, giving you a replica of popular birds from around the globe.

A brief note about the perches: The parts and pieces for the perches on which the birds are displayed are included in the parts inventories for each bird. The instructions for building the perch for the northern cardinal, the red-capped robin-chat, the canary, the pink robin, and the sulphur-crested cockatoo are shown on pages 138 and 139. The instructions for building the perches for the Andean cock-of-the-rock and the scarlet macaw are included with the instructions for those birds.

I hope you enjoy creating each bird as much as I enjoyed making them all. Happy building!

CONTENTS

NORTHERN CARDINAL

Cardinalis cardinalis

The male northern cardinal (*Cardinalis cardinalis*) was an obvious choice when choosing birds to build in my North American series. Its brilliant red plumage and distinctive crest make it instantly recognizable. This was one of my most difficult birds to build. It took me several attempts to replicate its distinctive head and crest.

- The northern cardinal is the official bird of no fewer than seven U.S. states and is well-loved by Americans. It frequently appears on postage stamps.

- They don't migrate and were more common in the warmer areas of the U.S. southeast but in recent decades they have expanded their range through the U.S. and even into Canada, perhaps due to their ability to adapt to parks and suburban human habitats.

- They were once popular as a pet but its sale as a cage bird is now banned.

- They are predominantly monogamous and mate for life.

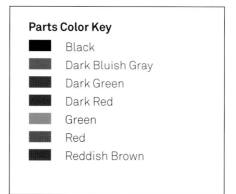

Parts Color Key

■ Black
■ Dark Bluish Gray
■ Dark Green
■ Dark Red
■ Green
■ Red
■ Reddish Brown

For instructions on building the perch, see page 138.

8x
3024

3x
3666

2x
85984

2x
3795

4x
92946

1x
3795

2x
3048

1x
3032

2x
3040b

1x
3958

4x
32062

2x
3035

1x
6538a

1x
54200

2x
32016

28x
54200

1x
32039

32x
54200

4x
2420

2x
3022

1x
3623

1x
3623

6x
3623

6x
3021

3x
3710

2x
3710

2x
3020

7x
3020

2x
30414

1x
44567

1x
44302

2x
3024

5x
15573

6x
3794b

2x
3023

16x
3023

12x
3023

1x
2420

3x
63864

6x
2431

2x
41769

2x
41770

1x
87087

2x
4733

4x
47905

1x
3941

1x
3004

1x
63965

1x
3070b

2x
2555

1x
3069b

2x
3069b

2x
3069b

1x
3068b

1x
3068b

1x
30374

1

2

3

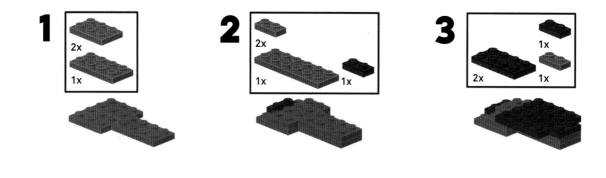

4

5

6

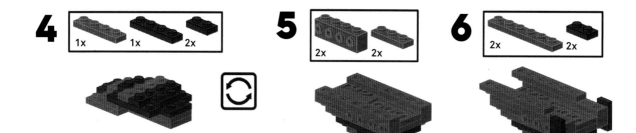

7

8

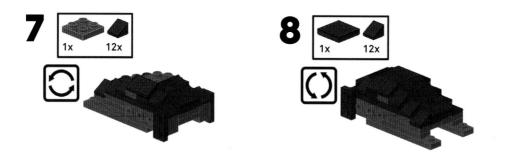

9

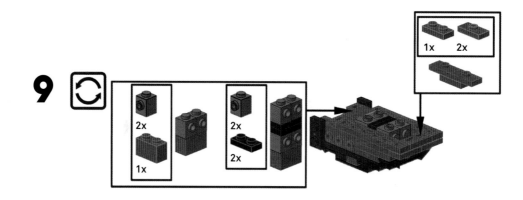

1 1x

2 2x 2x 2x 2x

3 4x 8x

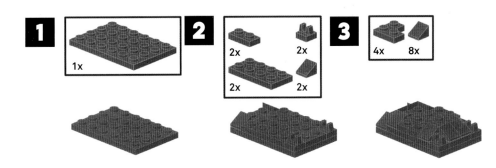

4 1x 8x

5 2x 1x

6 1x 2x 1x

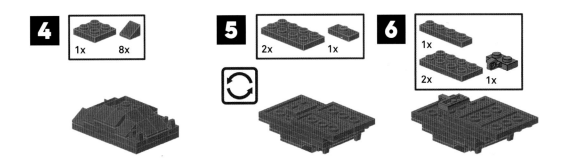

7 1x 8x

10

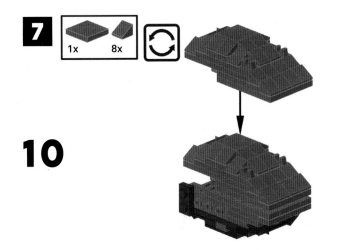

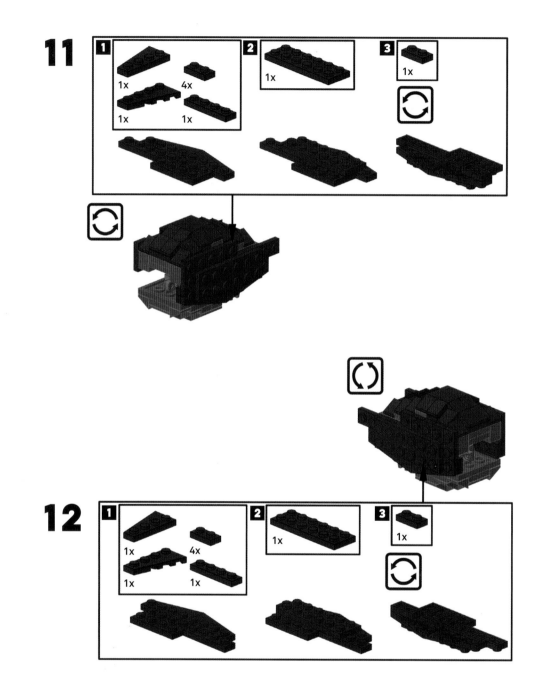

1

2x 1x

2

1x

1 1x 1x **2** 1x **3** 1x

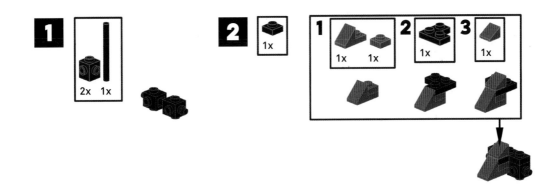

3

2x

1 1x 1x **2** 1x 2x **3** 1x 1x

4 1x 1x **5** 1x 1x **6** 2x

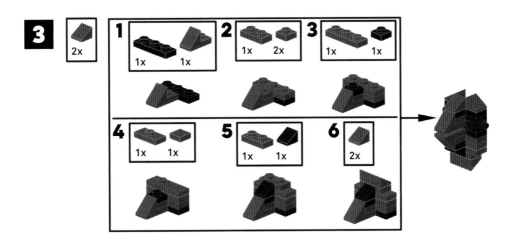

4

2x

1 1x 1x **2** 1x 1x **3** 1x 1x **4** 1x 1x **5** 3x

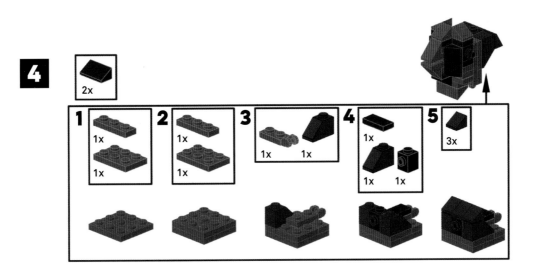

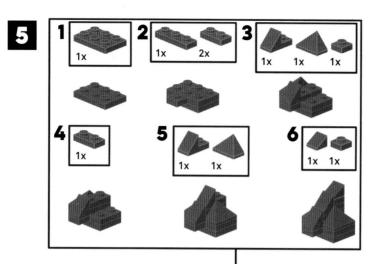

13

14

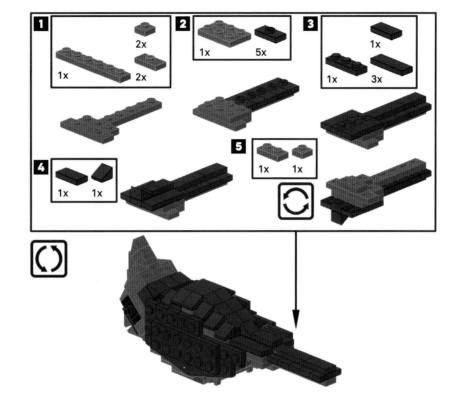

15

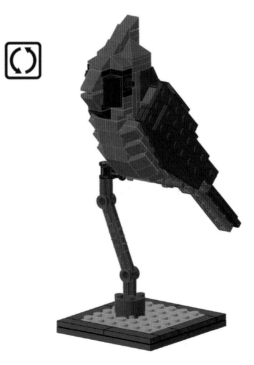

COMMON GRACKLE

Quiscalus quiscula

The common grackle (*Quiscalus quiscula*) looks like a blackbird that's been slightly stretched, and has a glossy iridescent body. I love the hints of green and purple in its plumage and this is the reason why I built it.

- They are found in large numbers in North America and Canada, and farmers consider them a pest because of their liking for corn. They forage in large flocks.

- They can often be seen at bird feeders, attracted by grain or seed, and will push other birds aside.

- They roost at night in high trees or on power lines.

- They nest high in trees in loose colonies of up to 200 pairs, often near water.

Parts Color Key

- Black
- Blue
- Dark Bluish Gray
- Dark Purple
- Green
- Light Bluish Gray
- Yellow

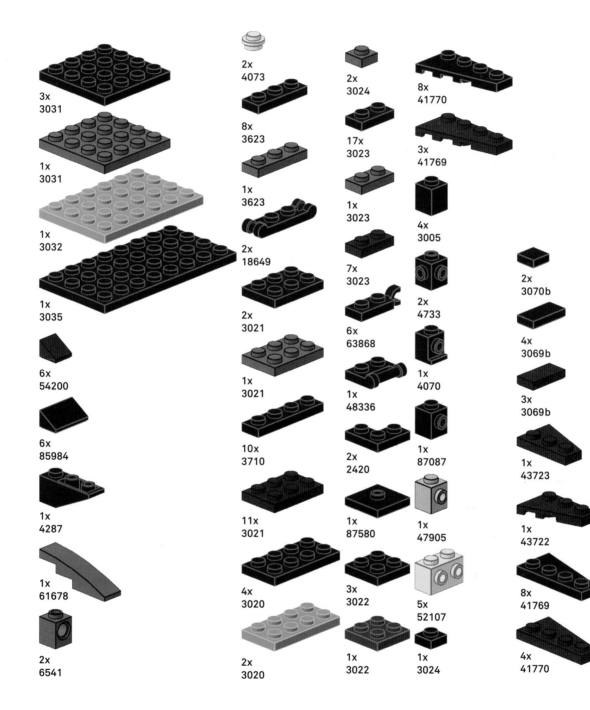

3x
3031

1x
3031

1x
3032

1x
3035

6x
54200

6x
85984

1x
4287

1x
61678

2x
6541

2x
4073

8x
3623

1x
3623

2x
18649

2x
3021

1x
3021

10x
3710

11x
3021

4x
3020

2x
3020

2x
3024

17x
3023

1x
3023

7x
3023

6x
63868

1x
48336

2x
2420

1x
87580

3x
3022

1x
3022

8x
41770

3x
41769

4x
3005

2x
4733

1x
4070

1x
87087

1x
47905

5x
52107

1x
3024

2x
3070b

4x
3069b

3x
3069b

1x
43723

1x
43722

8x
41769

4x
41770

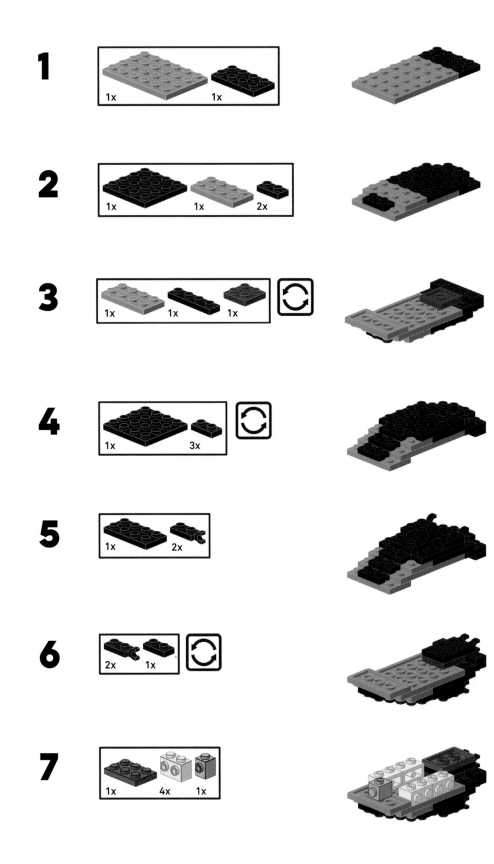

1
1x 1x

2
1x 1x 2x

3
1x 1x 1x

4
1x 3x

5
1x 2x

6
2x 1x

7
1x 4x 1x

8

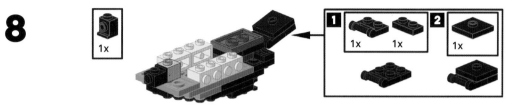

9

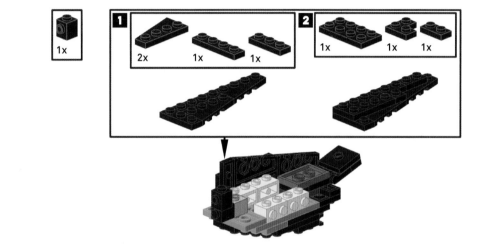

10

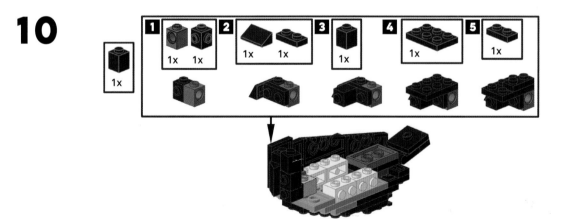

11

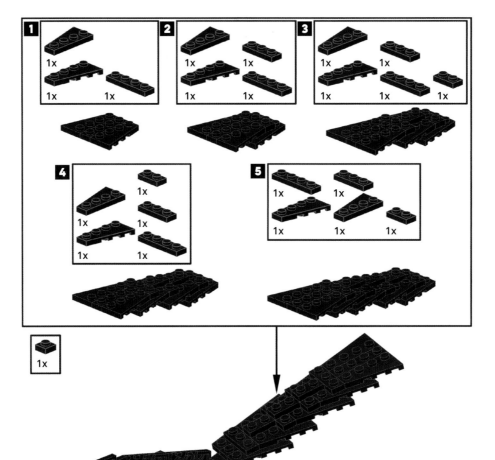

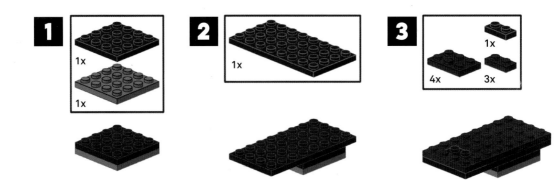

4
2x
1x
1x
1x
2x

5
2x
1x
1x

6
2x
1x
1x

7
1x
1x
1x

12
2x

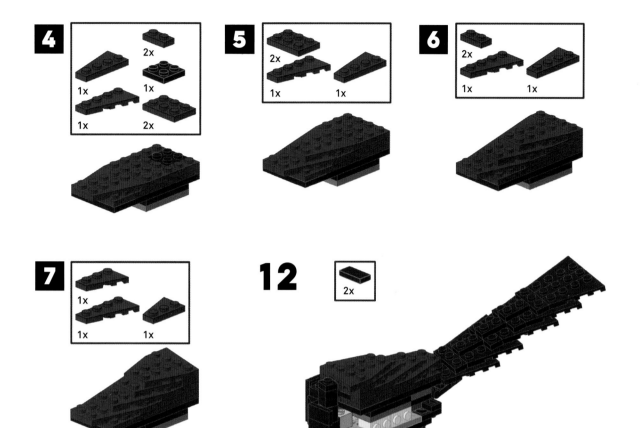

13

1 1x 1x

2 1x 1x

3 1x

4 1x

5 1x

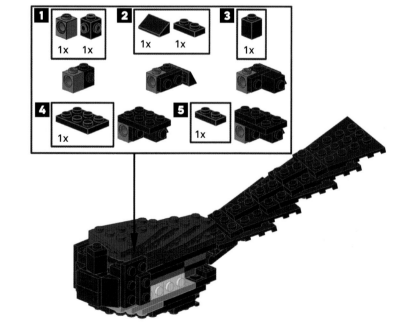

14

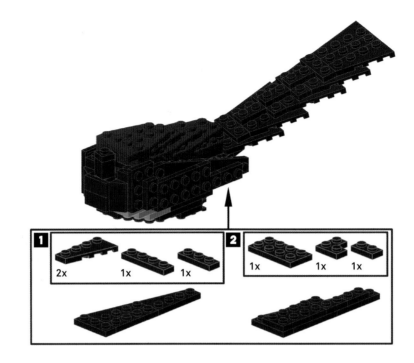

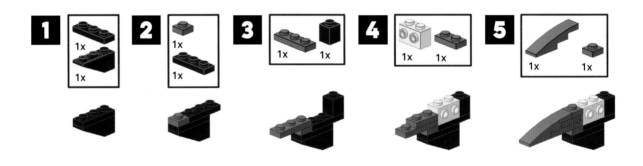

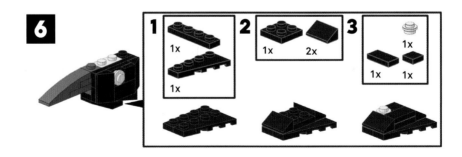

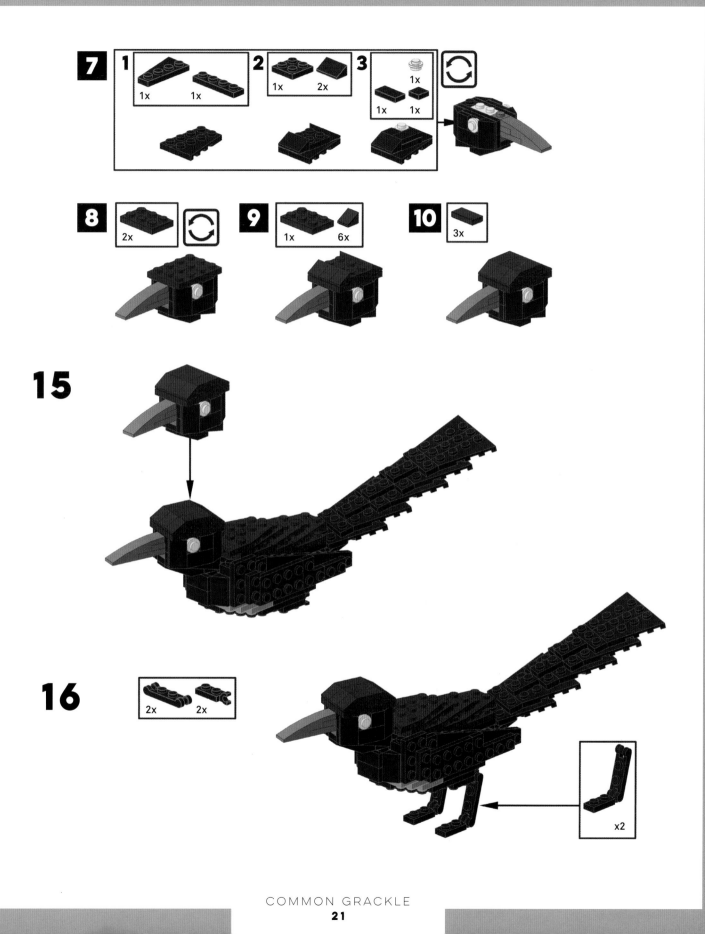

PAINTED BUNTING

Passerina ciris

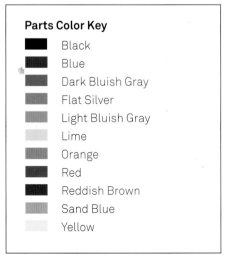

The male painted bunting (*Passerina ciris*) is thought by many to be the most beautiful bird in North America. The amazing, vibrant reds, greens, and blues of its plumage inspired me to recreate it in LEGO.

- A songbird belonging to the cardinal family, the painted bunting is a medium-sized finch, about 4¾ to 5½ inches (12 to 14 cm) long. It has a stubby bill for eating seeds but it also eats insects.

- It spends the summer months in northern Mexico and the southern United States, migrating to southern Mexico and Central America for the winter.

- This bird is fairly common, and although it is a shy, secretive bird, preferring dense vegetation, it is quite often found in suburban areas, and will be attracted by bird feeders.

- It has a warbling type of song, particularly noticeable in spring when the male is establishing its territory.

- Painted buntings have often been trapped and sold as cage birds. Despite the best efforts of conservationists, there is still an illegal trade in these stunning birds.

Parts Color Key

- Black
- Blue
- Dark Bluish Gray
- Flat Silver
- Light Bluish Gray
- Lime
- Orange
- Red
- Reddish Brown
- Sand Blue
- Yellow

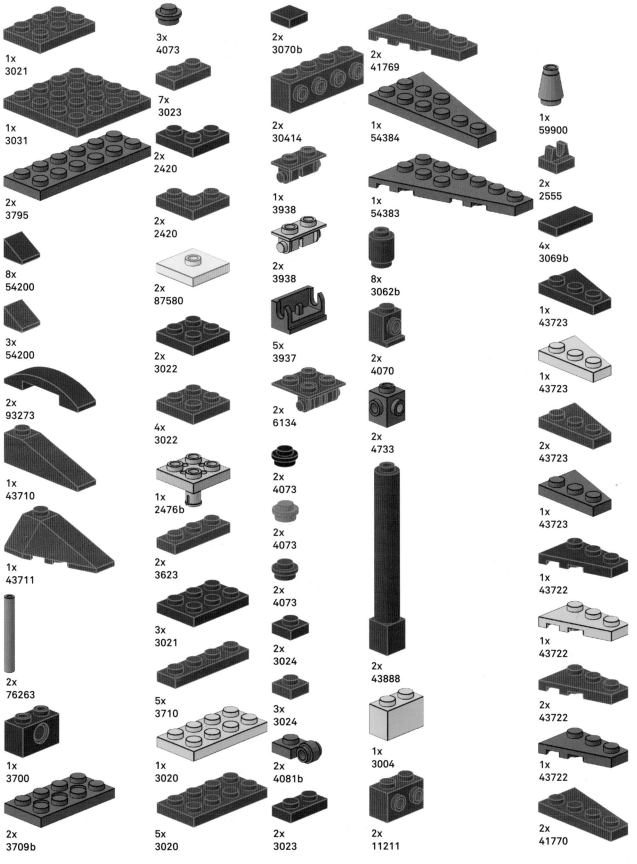

1x
3021

1x
3031

2x
3795

8x
54200

3x
54200

2x
93273

1x
43710

1x
43711

2x
76263

1x
3700

2x
3709b

3x
4073

7x
3023

2x
2420

2x
2420

2x
87580

2x
3022

4x
3022

1x
2476b

2x
3623

3x
3021

5x
3710

1x
3020

5x
3020

2x
3070b

2x
30414

1x
3938

2x
3938

5x
3937

2x
6134

2x
4073

2x
4073

2x
4073

2x
3024

3x
3024

2x
4081b

2x
3023

2x
41769

2x
54384

1x
54383

8x
3062b

2x
4070

2x
4733

2x
43888

1x
3004

2x
11211

1x
59900

2x
2555

4x
3069b

1x
43723

1x
43723

2x
43723

1x
43723

1x
43722

1x
43722

2x
43722

1x
43722

2x
41770

1

2

3

4

5

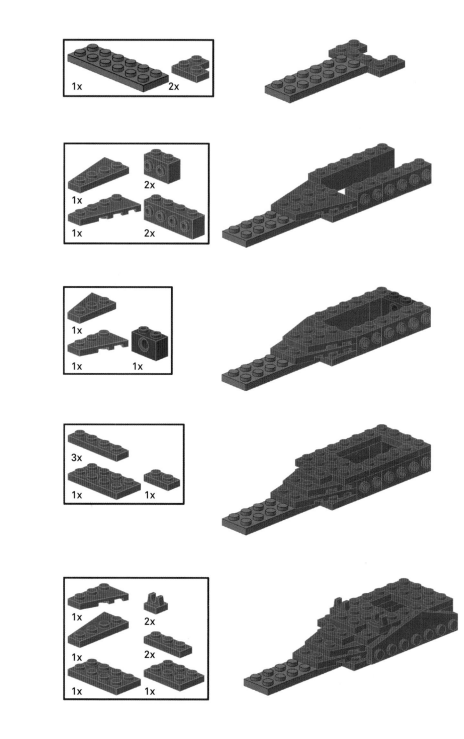

6

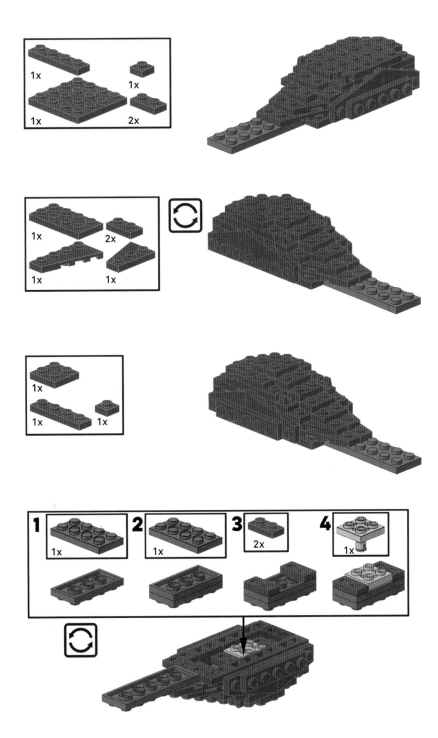

7

8

9

10

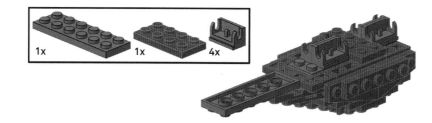

11

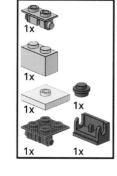

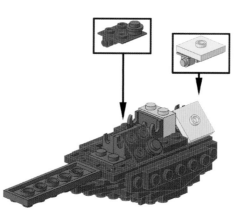

12

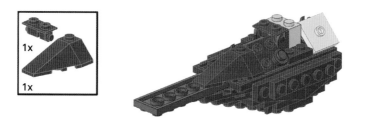

13

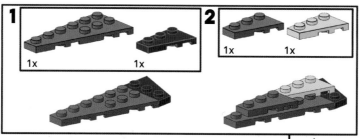

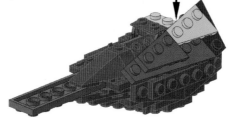

14

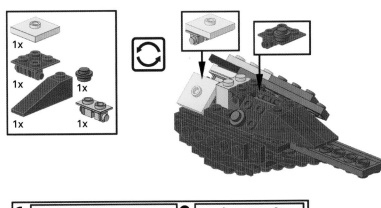

15

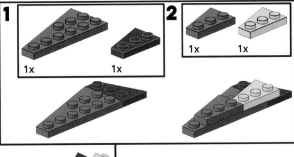

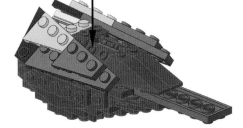

16

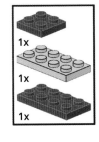

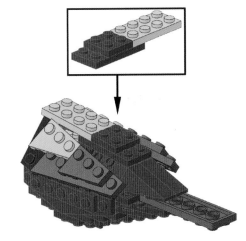

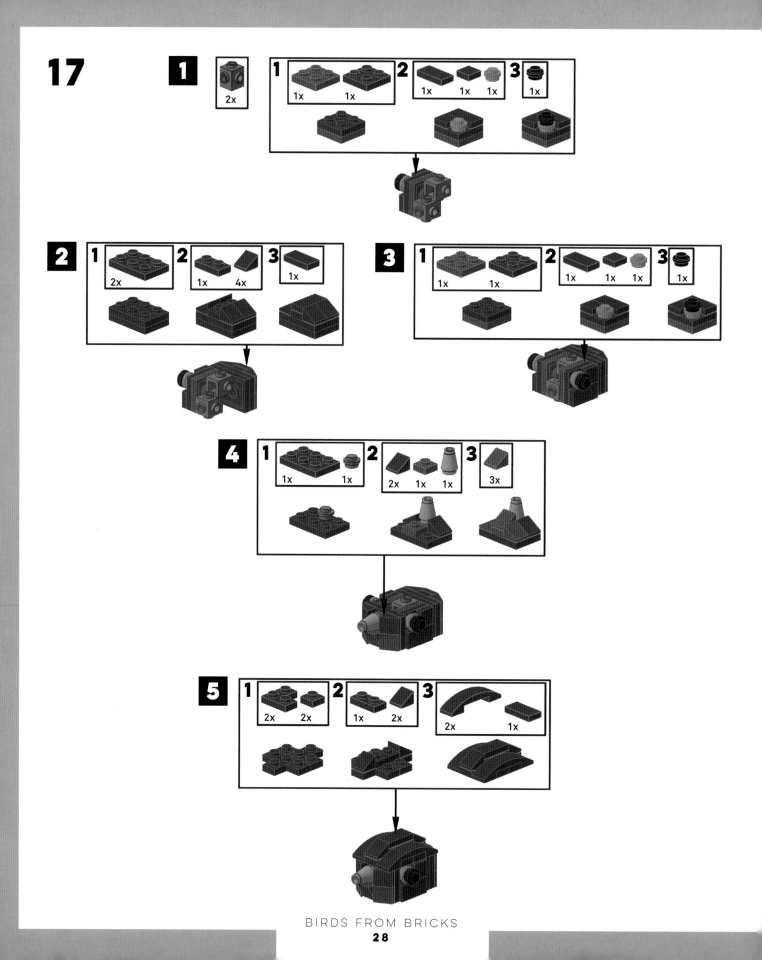

18

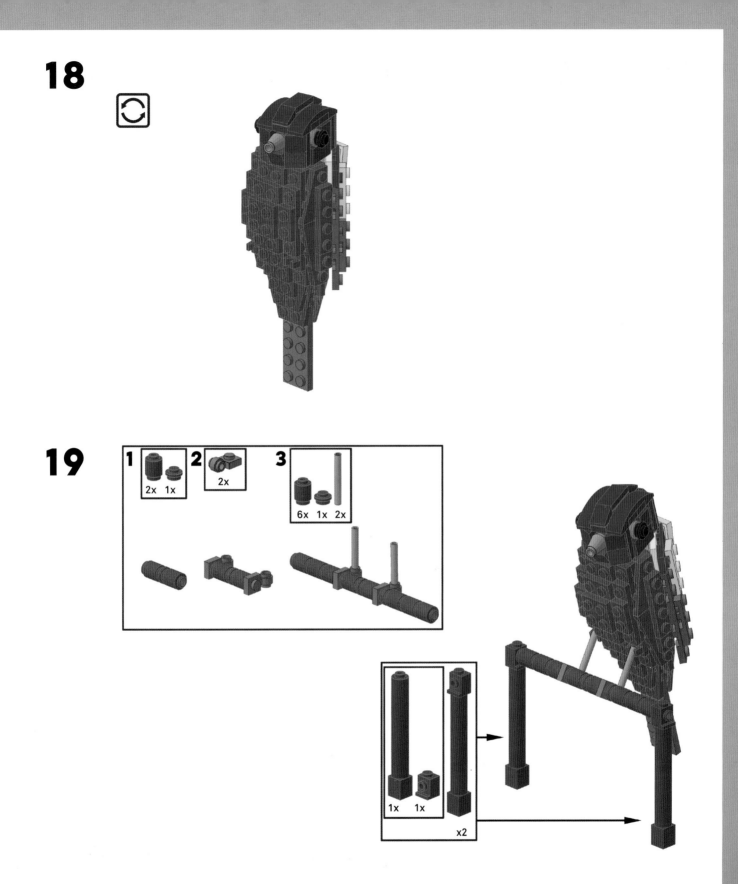

19

1 2x 1x
2 2x
3 6x 1x 2x

1x 1x

x2

ANDEAN COCK-OF-THE-ROCK
Rupicola Peruvianus

The Andean cock-of-the-rock (*Rupicola Peruvianus*) has remarkable plumage and is one of my South American collection. It's the national bird of Peru. The interesting crest shape is what attracted me to building it out of LEGO.

- The male is magnificent, with orange or red plumage on its head and neck areas, a prominent fan-shaped crest and black and grey wing and tail feathers. The female has no crest and is brown with hints of orange and red.

- They are found in the cloud forests of Peru and Ecuador, near rocky areas where they build their nests.

- They're not easy to spot, despite their bright color, being rather wary birds.

Parts Color Key

■	Black
■	Dark Bluish Gray
■	Dark Green
■	Green
■	Light Bluish Gray
■	Red
■	Reddish Brown
□	White
■	Yellow

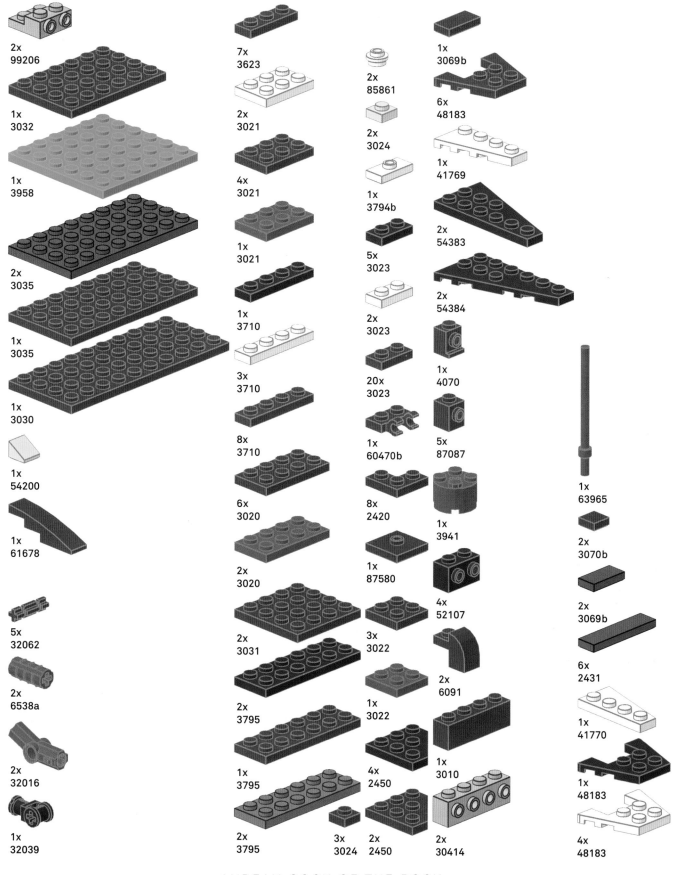

2x
99206

1x
3032

1x
3958

2x
3035

1x
3035

1x
3030

1x
54200

1x
61678

5x
32062

2x
6538a

2x
32016

1x
32039

7x
3623

2x
3021

4x
3021

1x
3021

1x
3710

3x
3710

8x
3710

6x
3020

2x
3020

2x
3031

2x
3795

1x
3795

2x
3795

3x
3024

2x
85861

2x
3024

1x
3794b

5x
3023

2x
3023

20x
3023

1x
60470b

8x
2420

1x
87580

3x
3022

1x
3022

4x
2450

2x
2450

1x
3069b

6x
48183

1x
41769

2x
54383

2x
54384

1x
4070

5x
87087

1x
3941

4x
52107

2x
6091

1x
3010

2x
30414

1x
63965

2x
3070b

2x
3069b

6x
2431

1x
41770

1x
48183

4x
48183

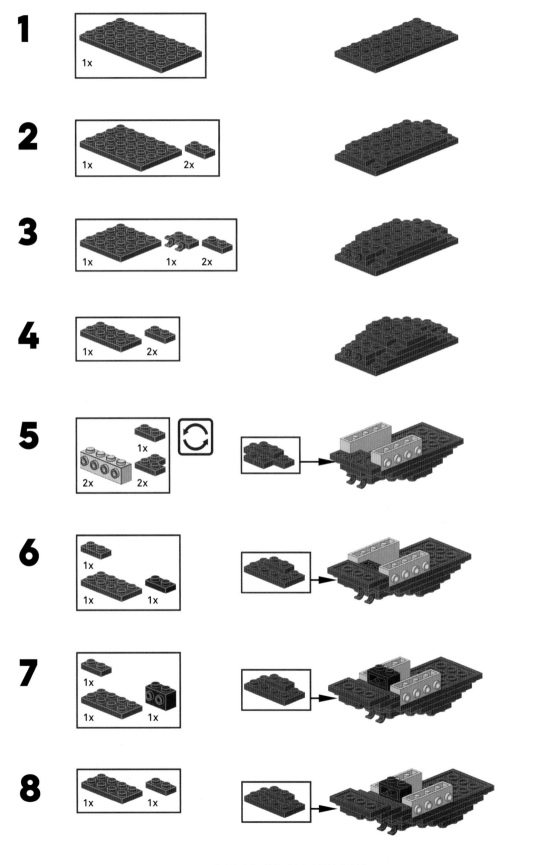

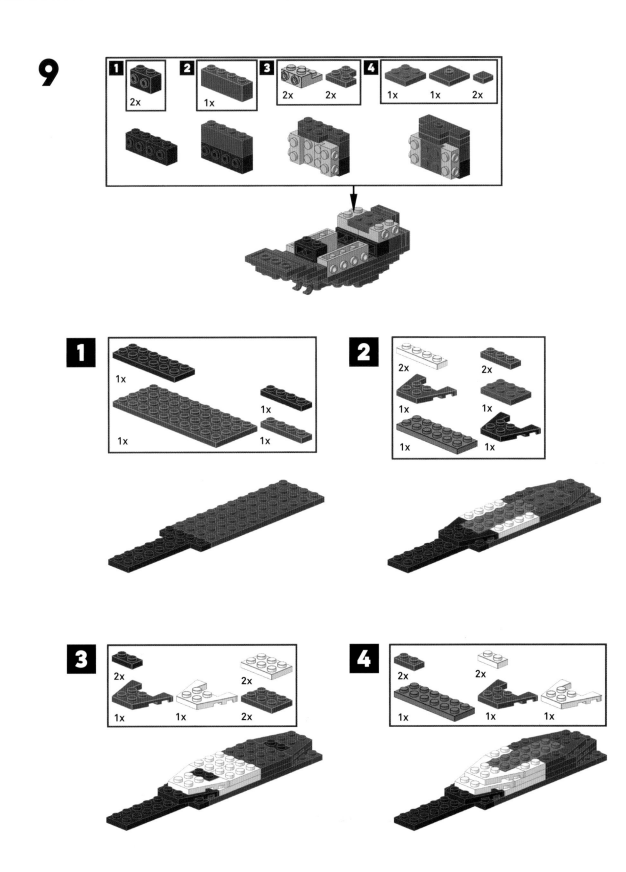

5

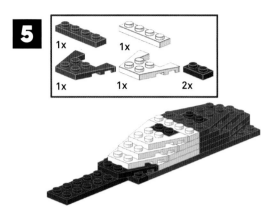

1x 1x
1x 1x 2x

6

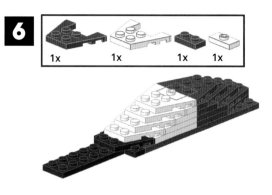

1x 1x 1x 1x

7

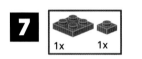

1x 1x

8

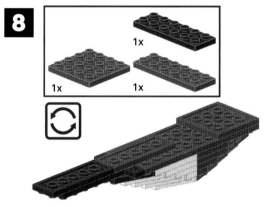

1x
1x 1x

9

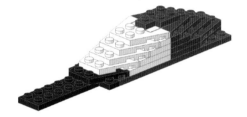

1x 2x

10

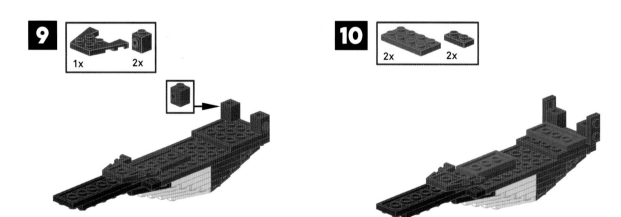

2x 2x

10

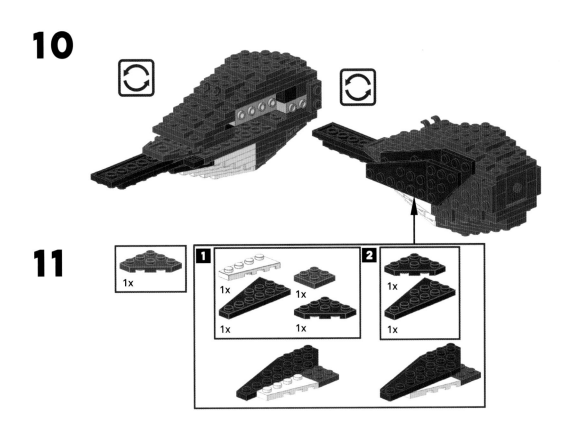

11

12

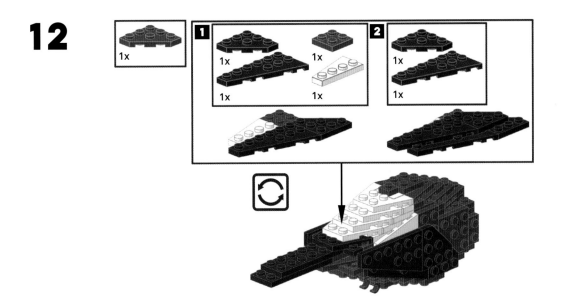

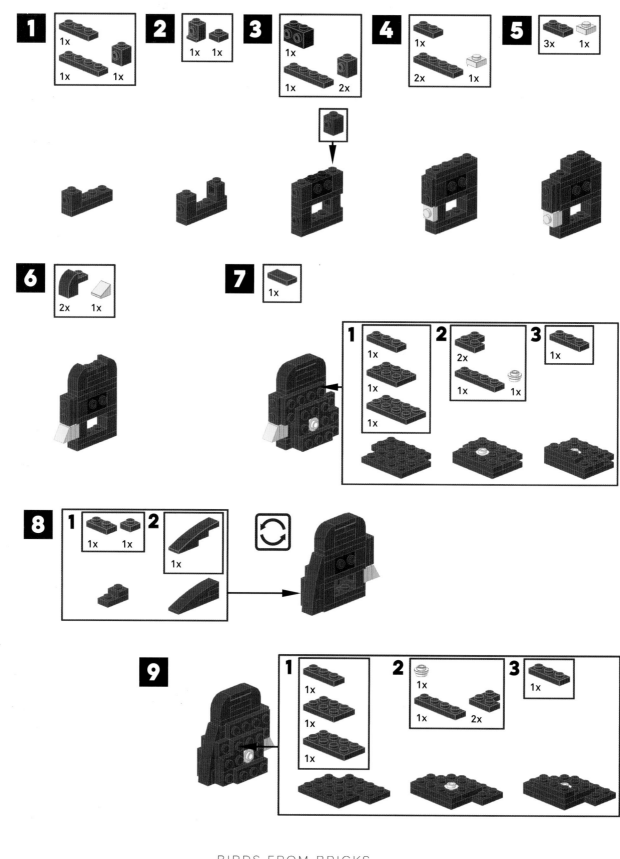

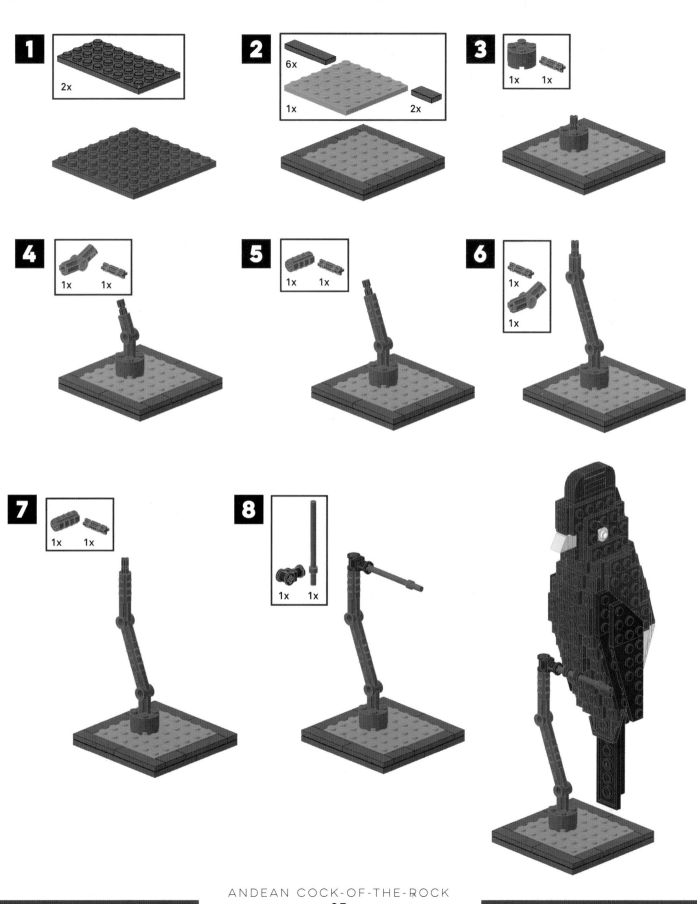

SCARLET MACAW

Ara macao

The scarlet macaw (*Ara macao*) is an attractive bird with distinctive red, blue, and yellow markings. The primary colors were easy to reproduce with LEGO bricks and it's one of my favorite bird builds.

- The scarlet macaw has a wingspan of around 3.3 feet (1 m), weighs around 2.2 pounds (1kg) and is the largest of the neotropical parrots. Their natural habitat is the South American rain forest.

- They usually mate for life and the female lays up to 4 eggs, with both parents caring for their young.

- In the wild they can live up to 50 years and in captivity they have been known to live up to 80 years, often outliving their owners!

- They are highly intelligent birds and popular as pets, which sadly means that there is much illegal trading in these wonderful birds, placing them on the endangered list.

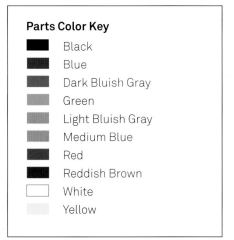

Parts Color Key

- ■ Black
- ■ Blue
- ■ Dark Bluish Gray
- ■ Green
- ■ Light Bluish Gray
- ■ Medium Blue
- ■ Red
- ■ Reddish Brown
- □ White
- ■ Yellow

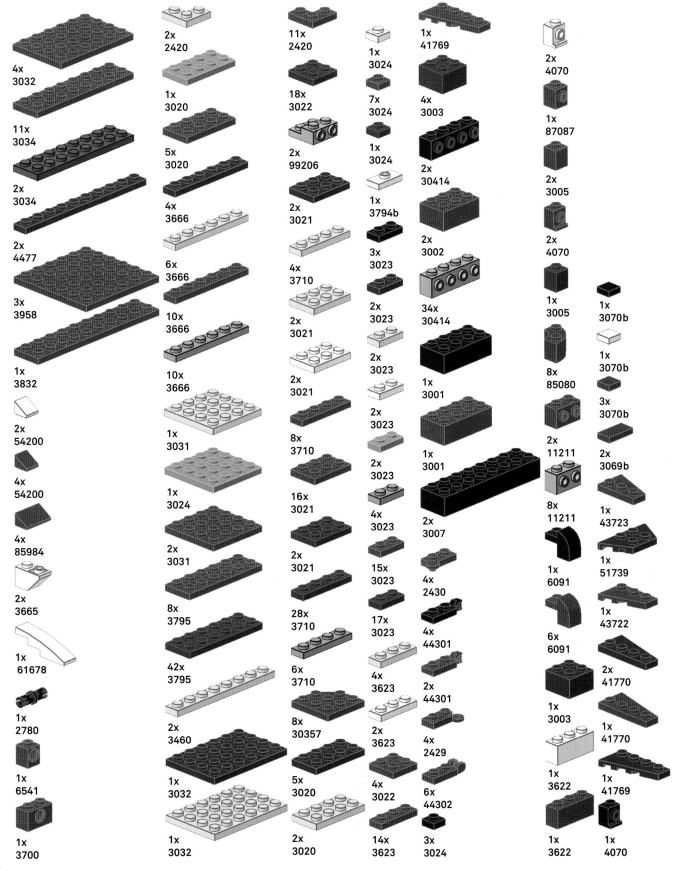

4x
3032

11x
3034

2x
3034

2x
4477

3x
3958

1x
3832

2x
54200

4x
54200

4x
85984

2x
3665

1x
61678

1x
2780

1x
6541

1x
3700

2x
2420

1x
3020

5x
3020

4x
3666

6x
3666

10x
3666

10x
3666

1x
3031

1x
3024

2x
3031

8x
3795

42x
3795

2x
3460

1x
3032

1x
3032

11x
2420

18x
3022

2x
99206

2x
3021

4x
3710

2x
3021

2x
3021

8x
3710

16x
3021

2x
3021

28x
3710

6x
3710

8x
30357

5x
3020

2x
3020

1x
3024

7x
3024

1x
3024

1x
3794b

3x
3023

2x
3023

2x
3023

2x
3023

2x
3023

4x
3023

15x
3023

17x
3023

4x
3623

2x
3623

4x
3022

14x
3623

1x
41769

4x
3003

2x
30414

2x
3002

34x
30414

1x
3001

1x
3001

2x
3007

4x
2430

4x
44301

2x
44301

4x
2429

6x
44302

3x
3024

2x
4070

1x
87087

2x
3005

2x
4070

1x
3005

8x
85080

2x
11211

8x
11211

1x
6091

6x
6091

1x
3003

1x
3622

1x
3070b

1x
3070b

3x
3070b

2x
3069b

1x
43723

1x
51739

1x
43722

2x
41770

1x
41770

1x
41769

1x
4070

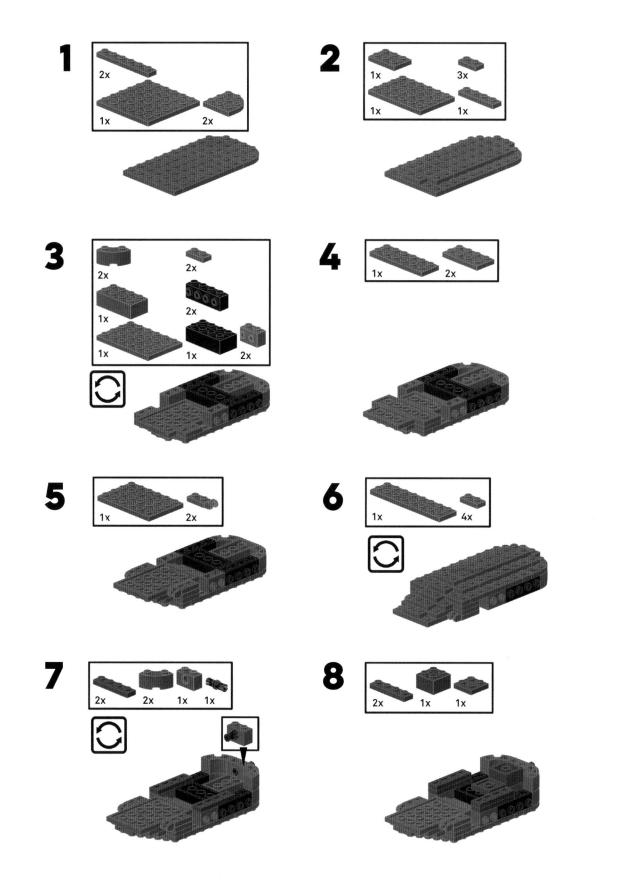

9

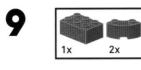

10

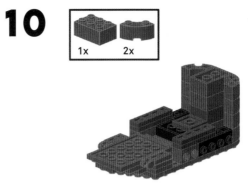

1

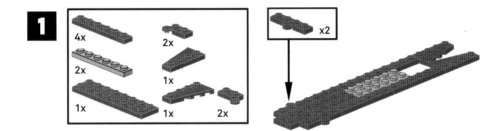

2

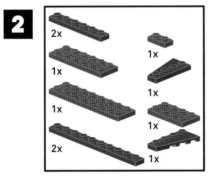

3

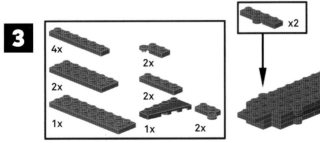

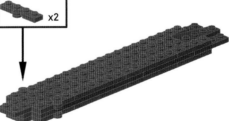

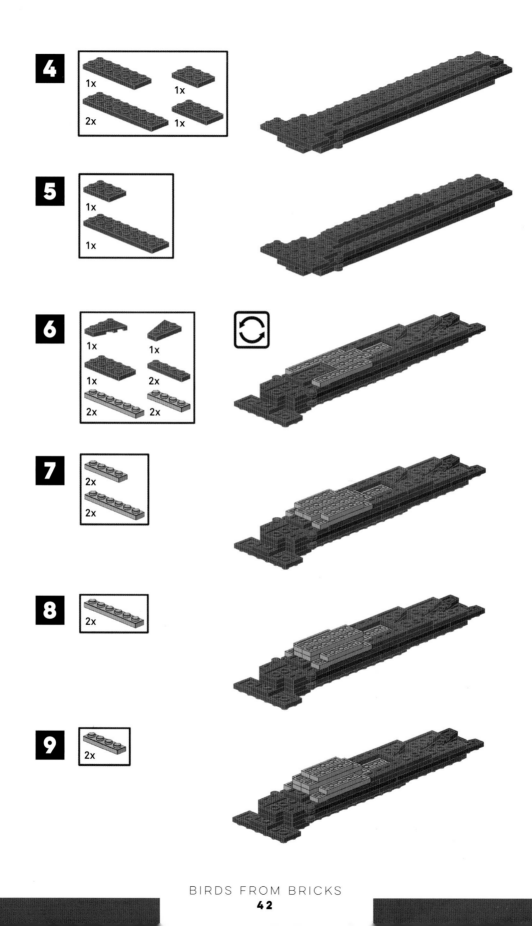

11

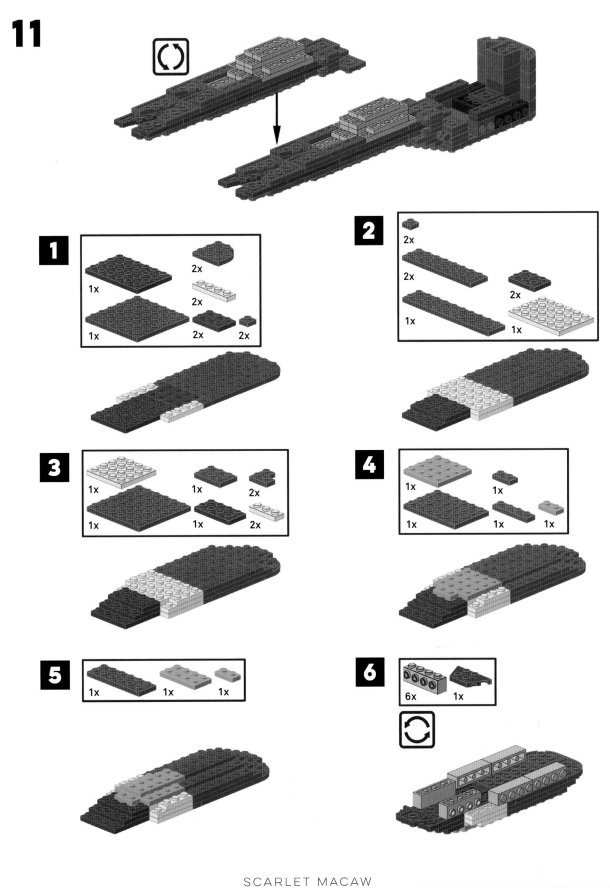

1 1x · 2x · 2x · 1x · 2x · 2x

2 2x · 2x · 2x · 1x · 2x · 1x

3 1x · 1x · 2x · 1x · 1x · 2x

4 1x · 1x · 1x · 1x · 1x · 1x

5 1x · 1x · 1x

6 6x · 1x

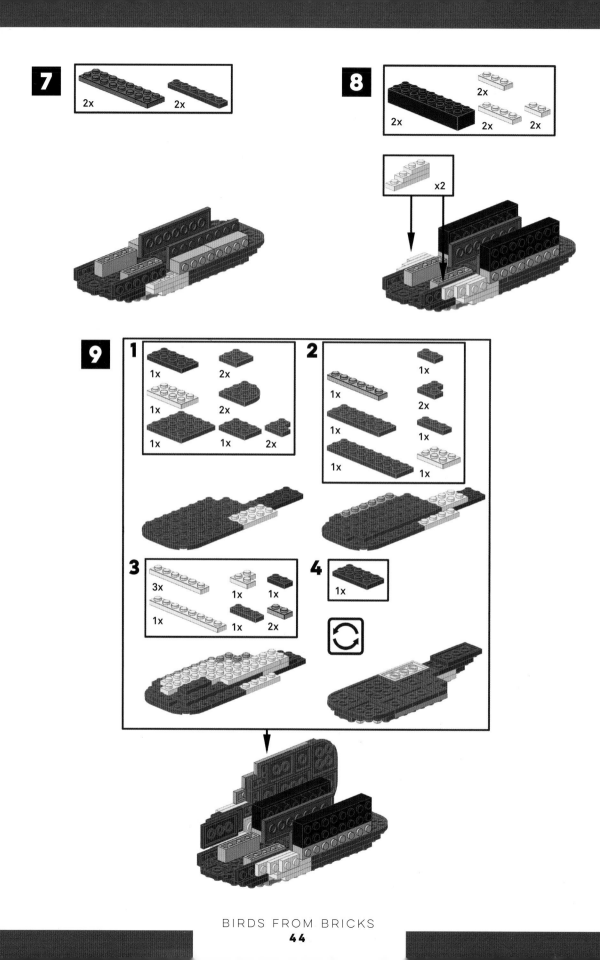

10

1
1x
2x
1x
2x
1x
1x
2x

2
1x
1x
1x
1x
1x
1x
1x
2x
1x

3
3x
1x
1x
1x
2x

4
1x

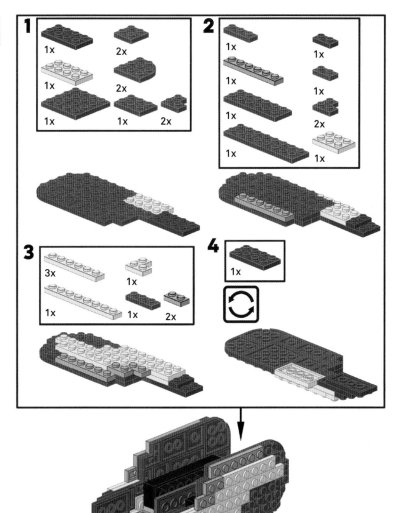

12

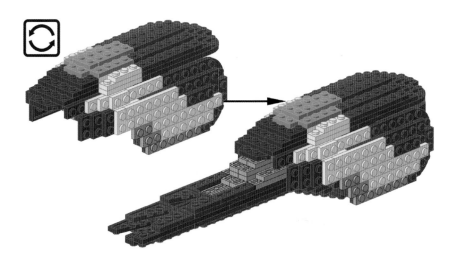

13

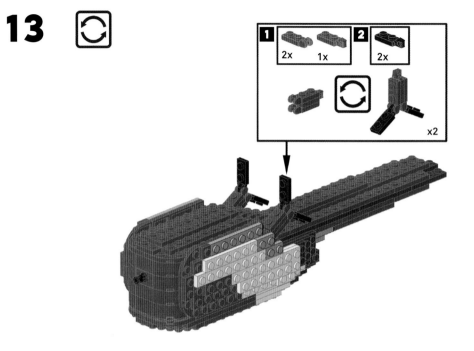

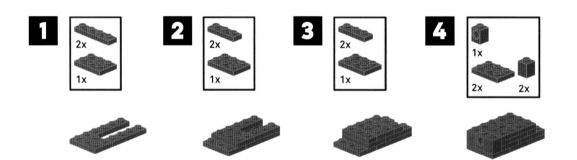

5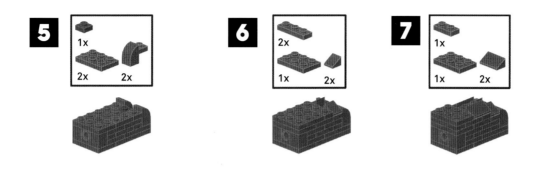

6

7

8

9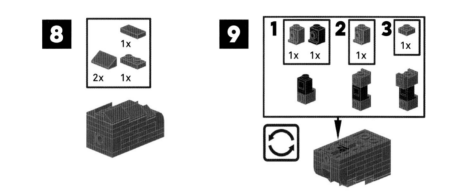

10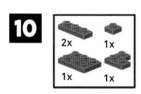

11

12

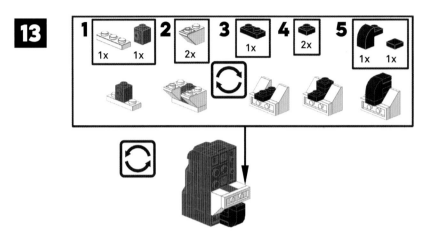

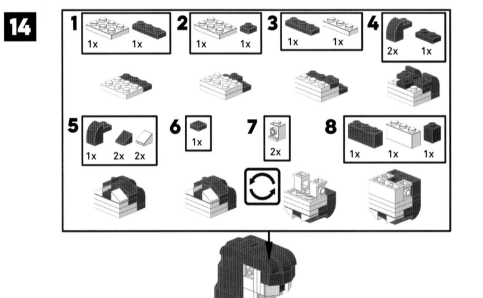

15

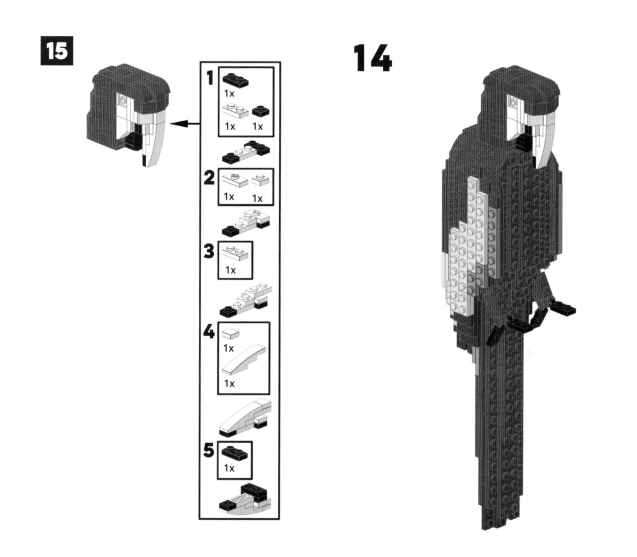

14

1

2x

4x   2x

2

5x

3

16x

4

6x

8x

5

5x   1x

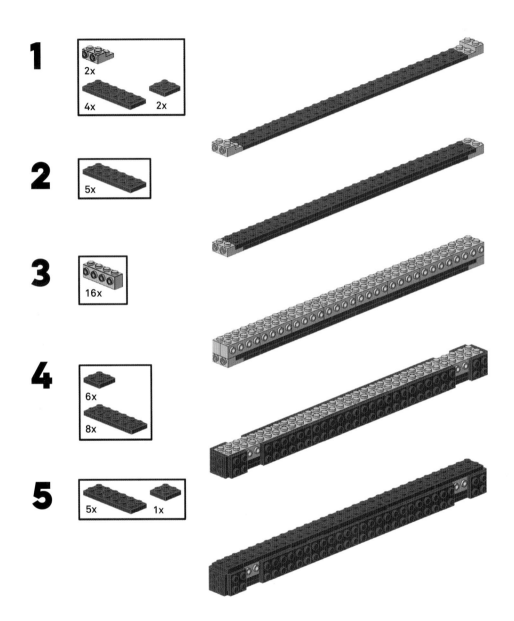

6

1 3x 6x 4x

2 3x 2x

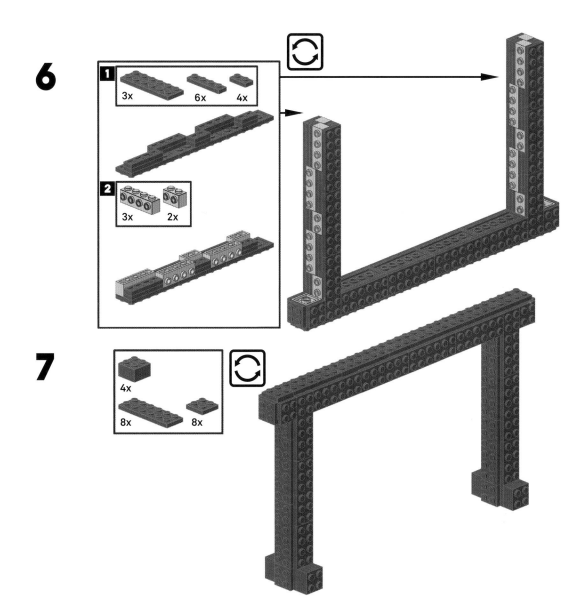

7 4x 8x 8x

NORTHERN ROCKHOPPER PENGUIN
Eudyptes c. Moseley

The northern rockhopper penguin (*Eudyptes c. Moseley*) breeds almost exclusively on Tristan da Cunha and Gough Island in the South Atlantic.

- The rockhopper breeds in colonies in a range of locations from sea level to cliffs, sometimes inland.

- It feeds on sea life such as krill, octopus, squid, fish, and crustaceans.

- It has a straight bright yellow eyebrow ending in long yellow plumes behind the eye. The top of the head has spiked black feathers.

- A study in 2009 showed that the nothern rockhopper world population had declined by 90 percent since the 1950s and it is now classified as endangered.

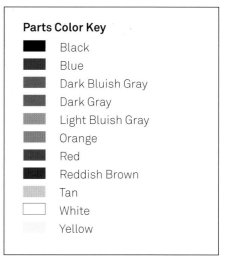

Parts Color Key

■	Black
■	Blue
■	Dark Bluish Gray
■	Dark Gray
■	Light Bluish Gray
■	Orange
■	Red
■	Reddish Brown
■	Tan
☐	White
■	Yellow

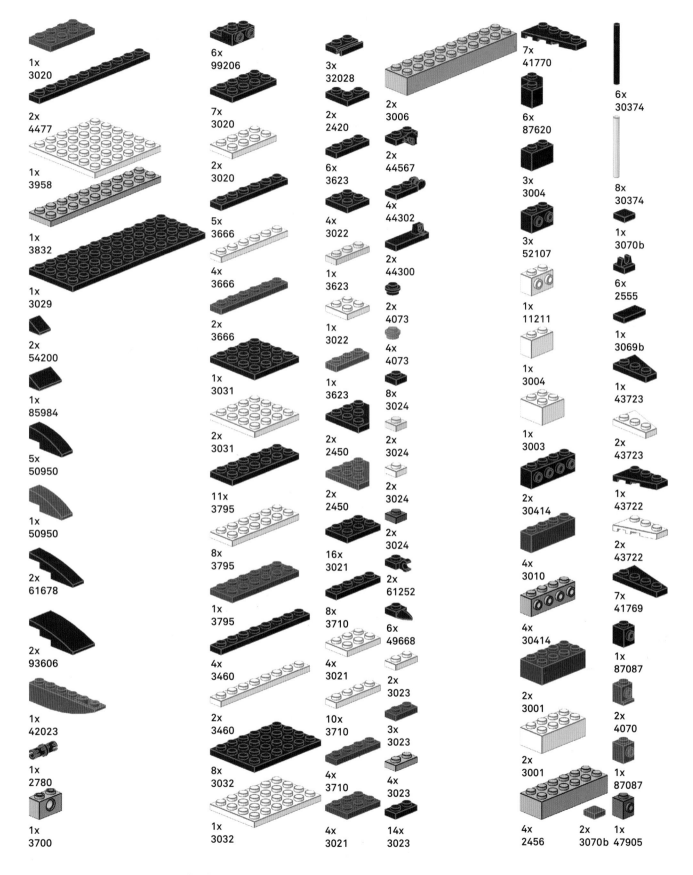

1x
3020

2x
4477

1x
3958

1x
3832

1x
3029

2x
54200

1x
85984

5x
50950

1x
50950

2x
61678

2x
93606

1x
42023

1x
2780

1x
3700

6x
99206

7x
3020

2x
3020

5x
3666

4x
3666

2x
3666

1x
3031

2x
3031

11x
3795

8x
3795

1x
3795

4x
3460

2x
3460

8x
3032

1x
3032

3x
32028

2x
2420

6x
3623

4x
3022

1x
3623

1x
3022

1x
3623

2x
2450

2x
2450

16x
3021

8x
3710

4x
3021

10x
3710

4x
3710

4x
3021

2x
3006

2x
44567

4x
44302

2x
44300

2x
4073

4x
4073

8x
3024

2x
3024

2x
3024

2x
3024

2x
61252

6x
49668

2x
3023

3x
3023

4x
3023

14x
3023

7x
41770

6x
87620

3x
3004

3x
52107

1x
11211

1x
3004

1x
3003

2x
30414

4x
3010

4x
30414

2x
3001

2x
3001

4x
2456

2x
3070b

1x
47905

6x
30374

8x
30374

1x
3070b

6x
2555

1x
3069b

1x
43723

2x
43723

1x
43722

2x
43722

7x
41769

1x
87087

2x
4070

1x
87087

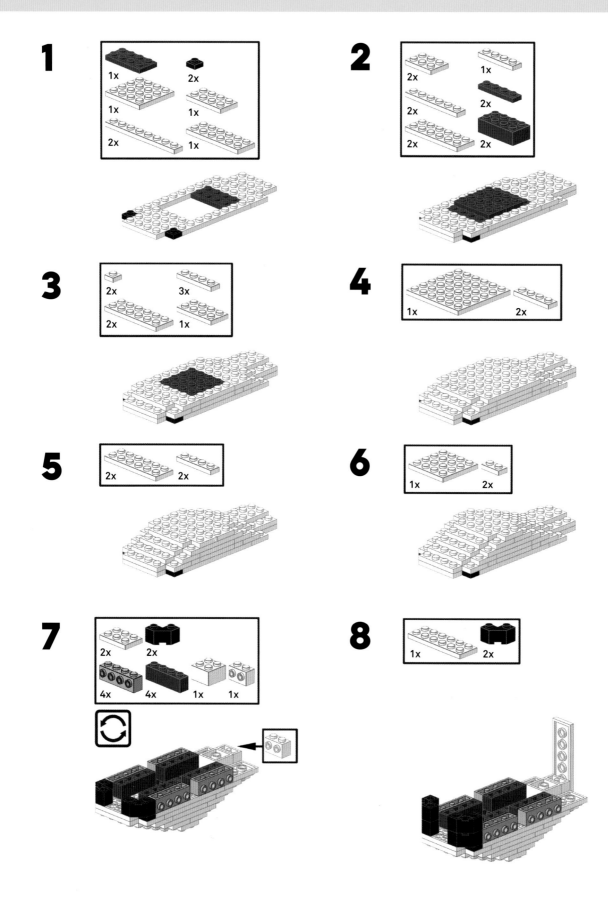

9

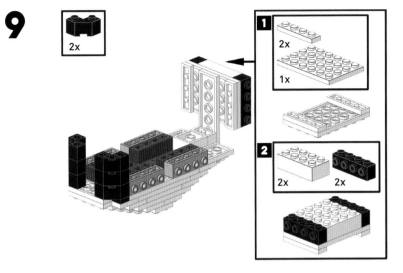

10

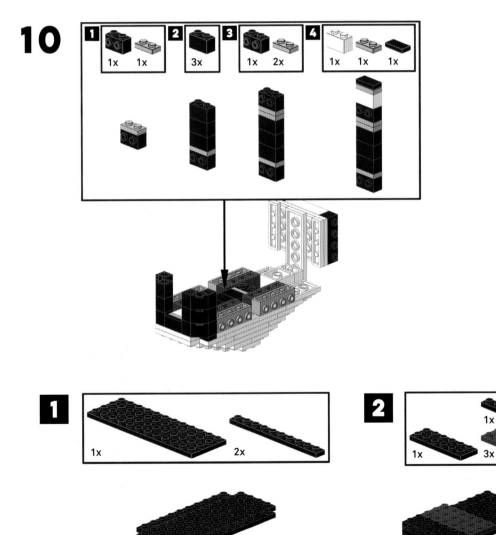

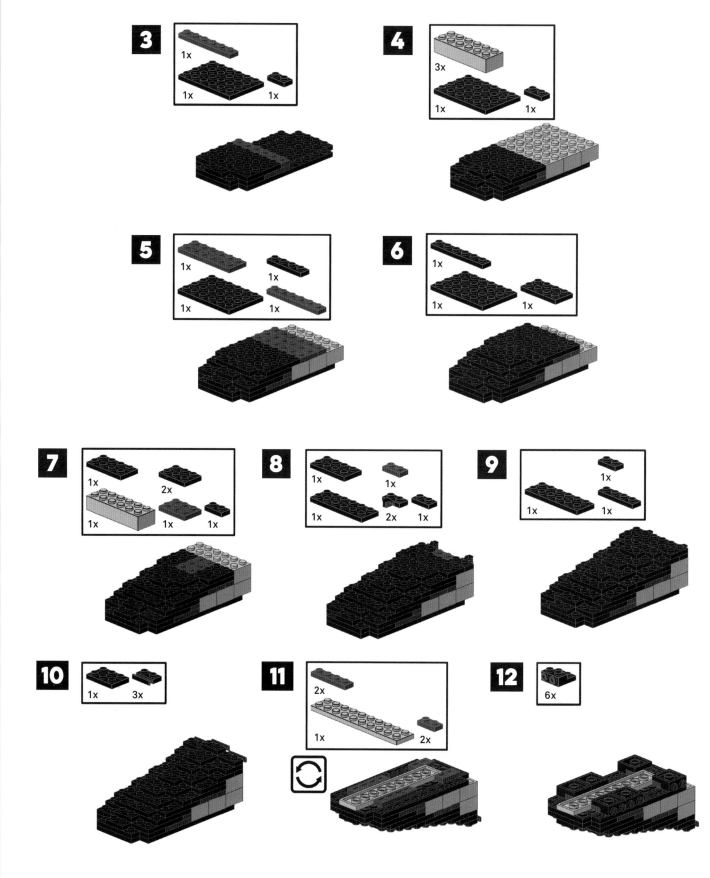

13 1x

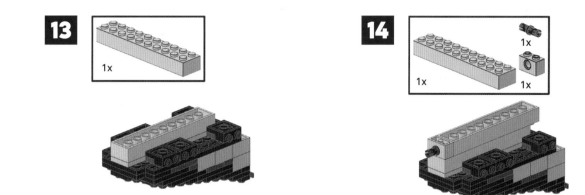

14 1x 1x 1x

11 ⟳

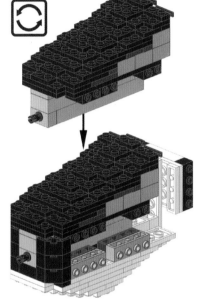

12 ⟳

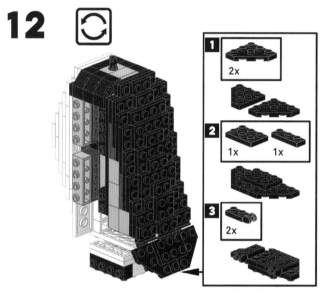

1 2x

2 1x 1x

3 2x

13 1x ⟳

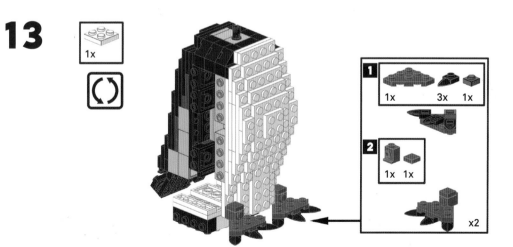

1 1x 3x 1x

2 1x 1x

x2

14

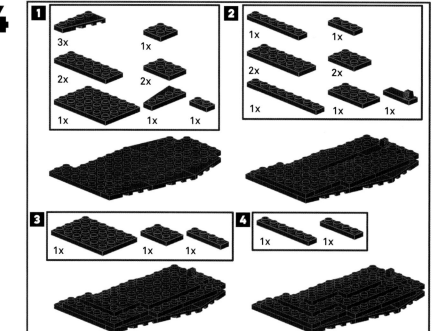

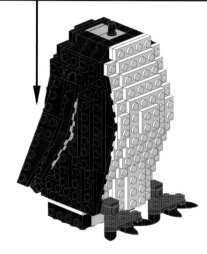

15

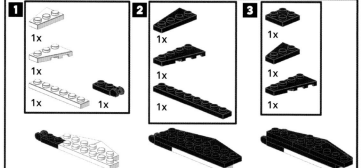

16

1
2x
2x
3x
2x
1x
1x
1x

2
1x
1x
2x
1x
1x
3x
1x

3
1x
2x
1x

4
1x
1x

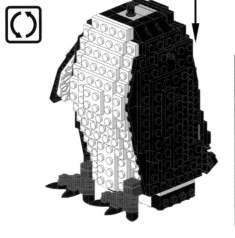

17

1
1x
1x
1x
1x

2
1x
1x
1x

3
1x
1x
1x
1x

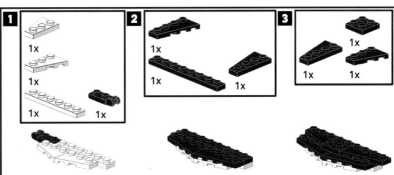

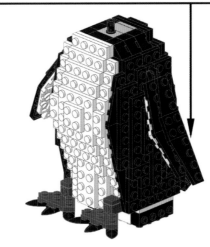

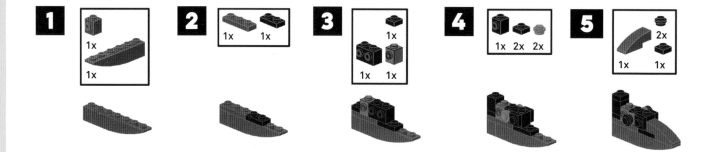

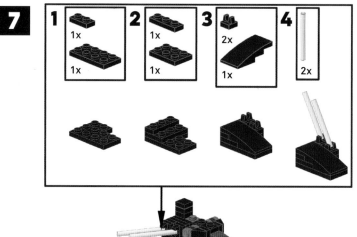

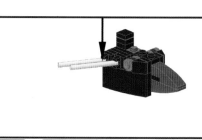

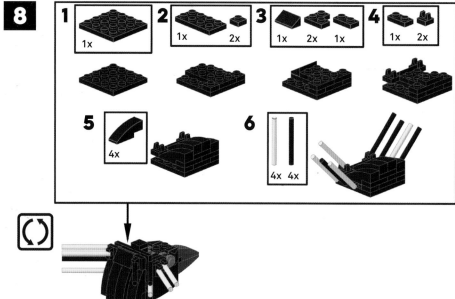

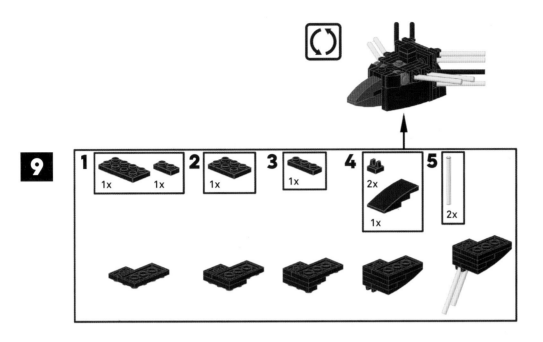

9

1 1x 1x
2 1x
3 1x
4 2x 1x
5 2x

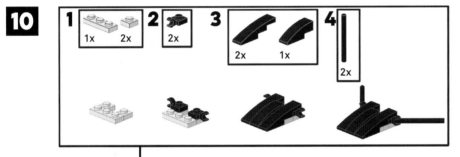

10

1 1x 2x
2 2x
3 2x 1x
4 2x

18

RED-CAPPED ROBIN-CHAT

Cossypha natalensis

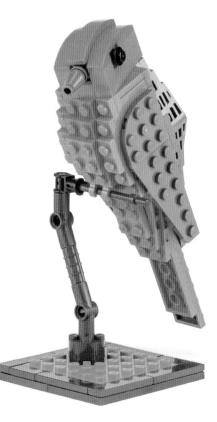

I built the red-capped robin-chat (*Cossypha natalensis*), formerly known as the Natal robin, because robins are one of my favorite species of bird and I wanted to build a lesser-known robin from Africa. I think the bright orange and dark gray is a beautiful combination of colors.

- The red-capped robin-chat is a small bird 6½ inches (16.5 cm) in length. The center of the back and wings are blue-gray in color, and the remainder of the plumage is rich orange-rufous.

- This bird has a loud warbling song and is an outstanding mimic of the songs and calls of other birds.

- Found widely distributed in East and Central and South Africa, it frequents dense forest undergrowth, woodlands, and coastal scrub, and is partially migratory in some areas.

- This shy, sulking species could be easily overlooked were it not for its loud song and calls.

Parts Color Key

- ■ Black
- ■ Dark Bluish Gray
- ■ Dark Green
- ■ Dark Tan
- ■ Green
- ■ Light Bluish Gray
- ■ Orange
- ■ Red
- ■ Reddish Brown

For instructions on building the perch, see page 138.

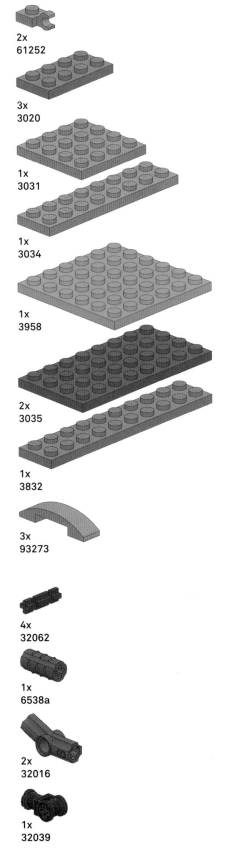

2x
61252

3x
3020

1x
3031

1x
3034

1x
3958

2x
3035

1x
3832

3x
93273

4x
32062

1x
6538a

2x
32016

1x
32039

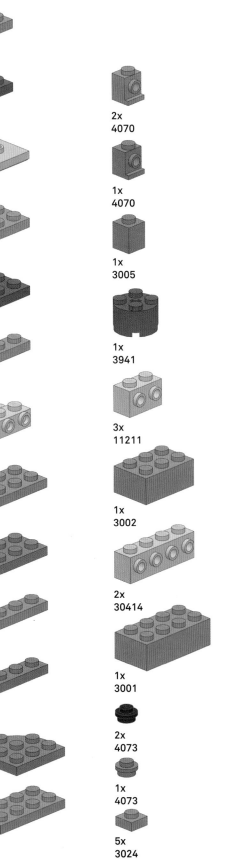

6x
3023

3x
3023

1x
87580

2x
3022

5x
3022

1x
3623

3x
99206

1x
3021

2x
3021

5x
3710

1x
3710

2x
30357

6x
3020

2x
4070

1x
4070

1x
3005

1x
3941

3x
11211

1x
3002

2x
30414

1x
3001

2x
4073

1x
4073

5x
3024

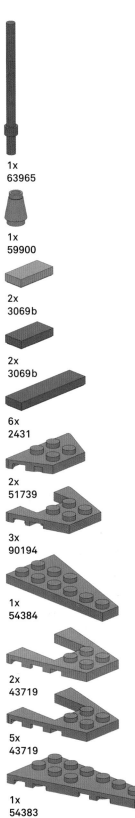

1x
63965

1x
59900

2x
3069b

2x
3069b

6x
2431

2x
51739

3x
90194

1x
54384

2x
43719

5x
43719

1x
54383

1

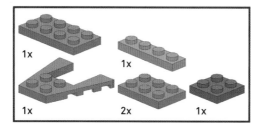

1x 1x
1x 2x 1x

2

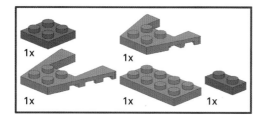

1x 1x
1x 1x 1x

3

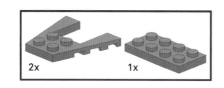

2x 1x

4

2x 1x

5

2x

6

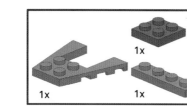

1x
1x 1x

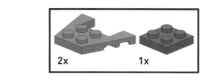

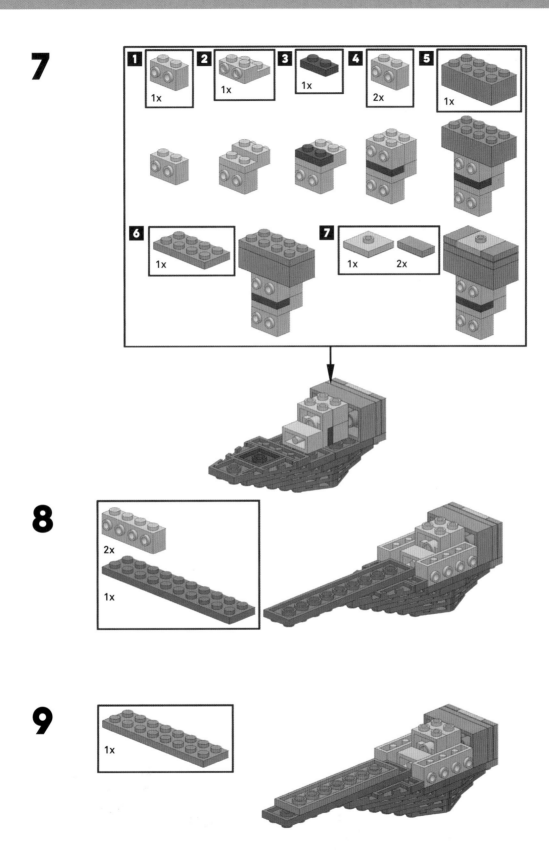

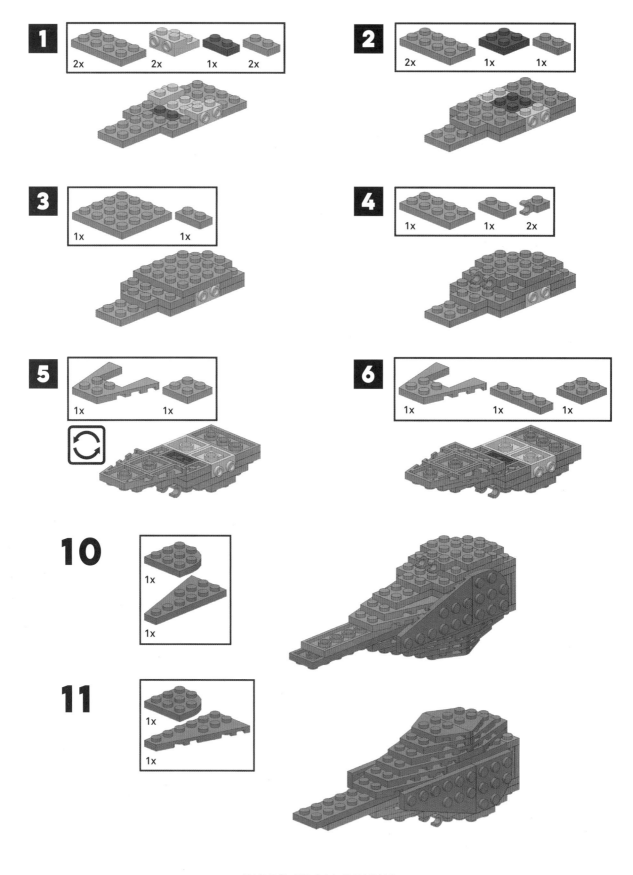

12

 1
3x

 2
1x   1x

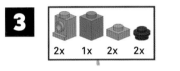

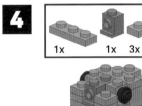

3
2x   1x   2x   2x

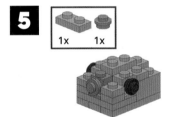

4
1x   1x   3x

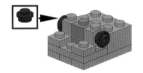

5
1x   1x

6
3x   1x

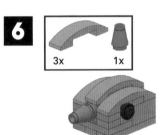

13

EURASIAN BLUE TIT

Cyanistes caeruleus

The blue tit (*Cyanistes caeruleus*) was the third bird that I built. I often see and hear it whilst gardening. My LEGO blue tit has appeared on television and in magazines and newspapers around the world, not to mention on the internet.

- The blue tit can be found throughout Europe and is particularly common in the U.K., where it is often seen on bird feeders in urban gardens all year round.

- It is an attractive small bird 4¾ inches (12 cm) in length with distinctive blue, yellow, white, and green plumage.

- They nest in tree holes but in urban areas they take advantage of nesting boxes and will return to the same box year after year.

- They are particularly agile and can often be seen hanging upside down on bird feeders.

Parts Color Key

■	Black
■	Blue
■	Dark Bluish Gray
■	Light Bluish Gray
■	Lime
■	Medium Blue
□	White
■	Yellow

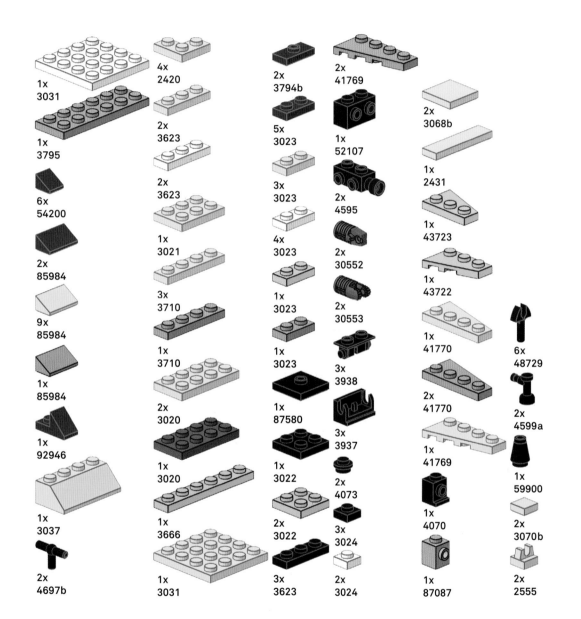

1x
3031

1x
3795

6x
54200

2x
85984

9x
85984

1x
85984

1x
92946

1x
3037

2x
4697b

4x
2420

2x
3623

2x
3623

1x
3021

3x
3710

1x
3710

2x
3020

1x
3020

1x
3666

1x
3031

2x
3794b

5x
3023

3x
3023

4x
3023

1x
3023

1x
3023

1x
87580

1x
3022

2x
3022

3x
3623

2x
41769

1x
52107

2x
4595

2x
30552

2x
30553

3x
3938

3x
3937

2x
4073

3x
3024

2x
3024

2x
3068b

1x
2431

1x
43723

1x
43722

1x
41770

2x
41770

1x
41769

1x
4070

1x
87087

6x
48729

2x
4599a

1x
59900

2x
3070b

2x
2555

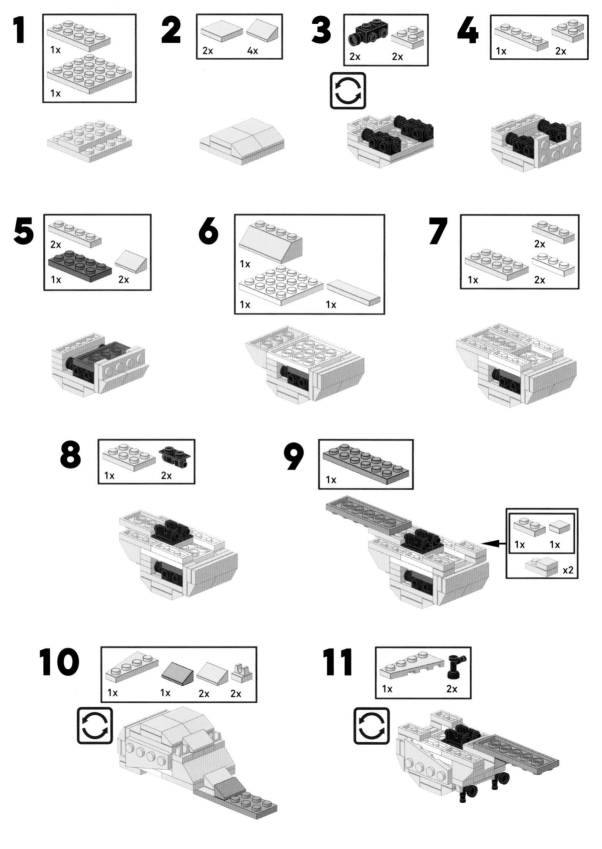

12

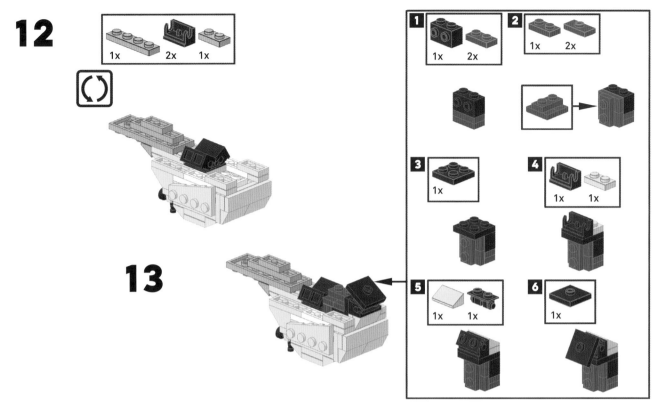

13

14

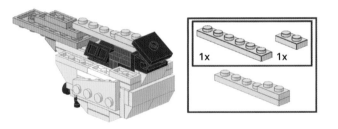

15

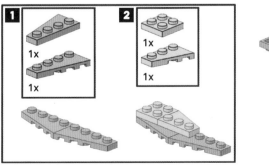

16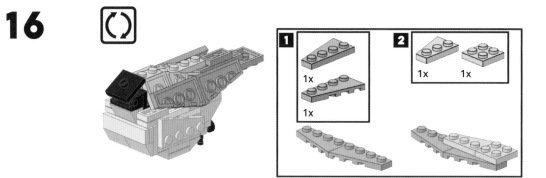

1 1x 1x

2 1x 1x

17

1 2x

2 1x 1x 2x

3 1x 2x 1x

4 2x 2x

5 2x 1x

6 1x

7 1x

8 5x

9 2x 2x

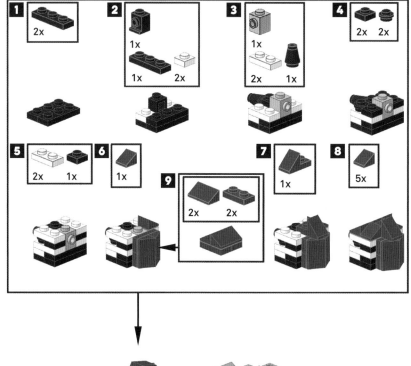

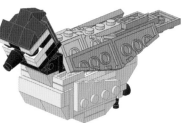

18

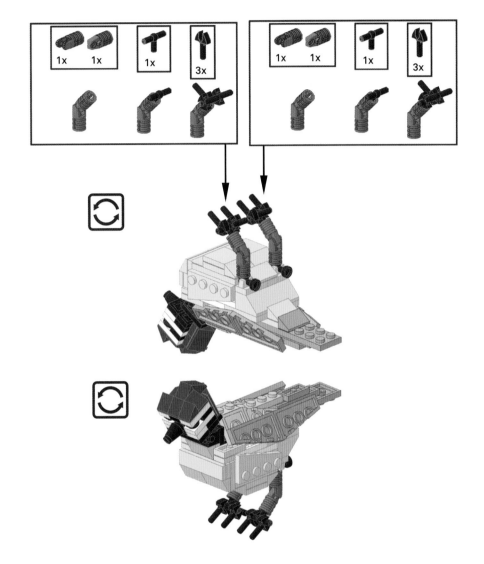

CANARY

Serinus canaria

The canary (*Serinus canaria*) has been bred in captivity for hundreds of years due to its attractive color variations and its pleasing song. The yellow canary is the most popular and was an easy choice for me to build in LEGO.

- A small songbird in the finch family, the domestic canary originates from the Canary Islands off the northwest coast of Africa. The bird is named after the islands.

- They were popular with European royalty and the upper classes in the 17th and 18th centuries and commanded high prices.

- They are favored by bird breeders around the world and there are many color variations.

Parts Color Key

■	Black
■	Blue
■	Dark Green
■	Green
■	Light Bluish Gray
■	Red
■	Reddish Brown
■	Tan
□	White
■	Yellow

For instructions on building the perch, see page 138.

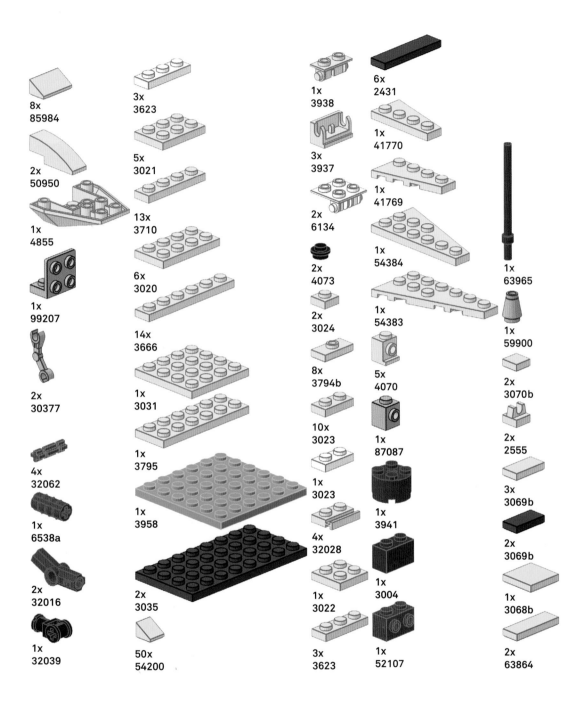

8x
85984

2x
50950

1x
4855

1x
99207

2x
30377

4x
32062

1x
6538a

2x
32016

1x
32039

3x
3623

5x
3021

13x
3710

6x
3020

14x
3666

1x
3031

1x
3795

1x
3958

2x
3035

50x
54200

1x
3938

3x
3937

2x
6134

2x
4073

2x
3024

8x
3794b

10x
3023

1x
3023

4x
32028

1x
3022

3x
3623

6x
2431

1x
41770

1x
41769

1x
54384

1x
54383

5x
4070

1x
87087

1x
3941

1x
3004

1x
52107

1x
63965

1x
59900

2x
3070b

2x
2555

3x
3069b

2x
3069b

1x
3068b

2x
63864

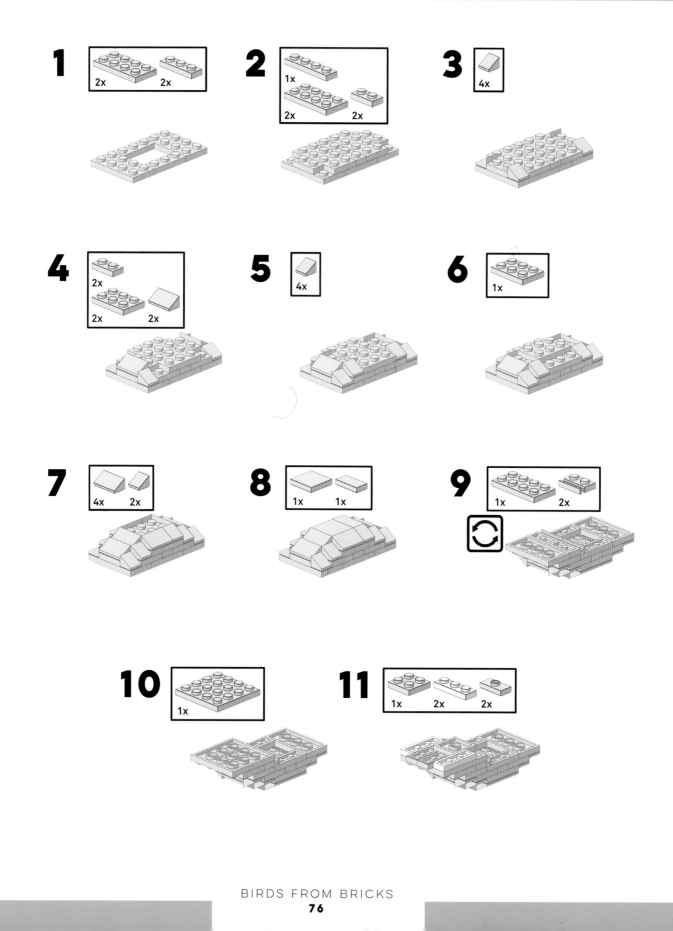

12

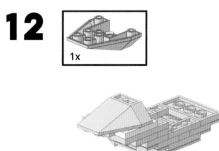

1x

13

1x 1x 2x

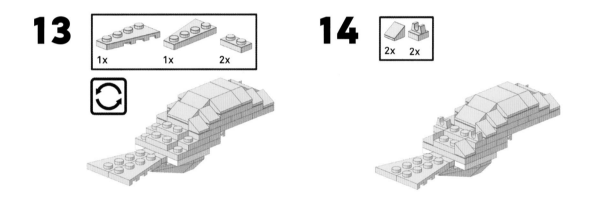

14

2x 2x

15

1x 1x

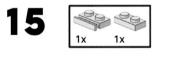

16

1x 2x

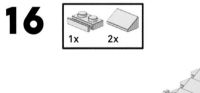

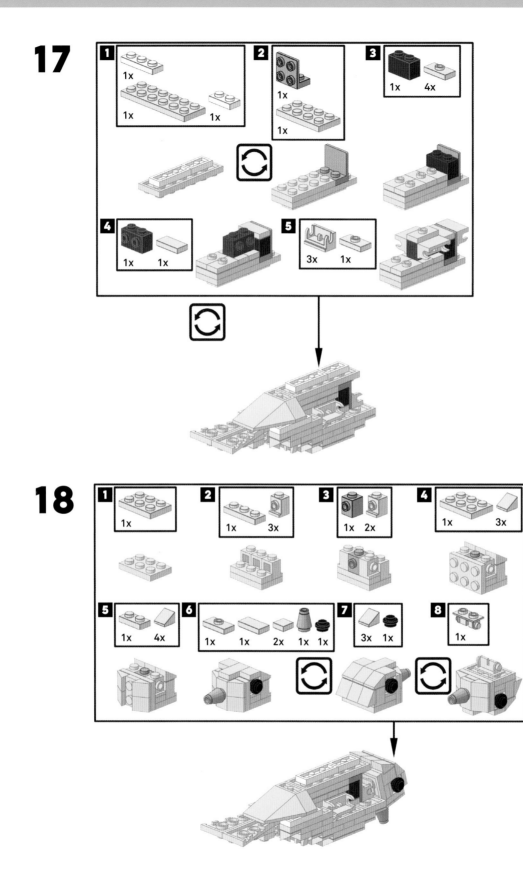

1

1x
1x
1x
2x

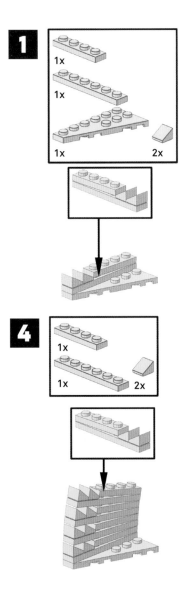

2

1x
1x
2x

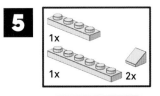
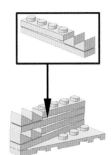

3

1x
1x
2x

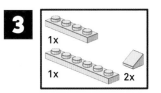
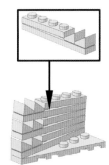

4

1x
1x
2x

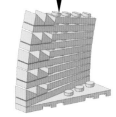

5

1x
1x
2x

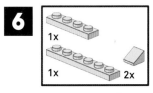
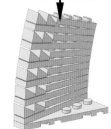

6

1x
1x
2x

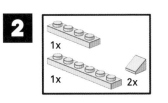

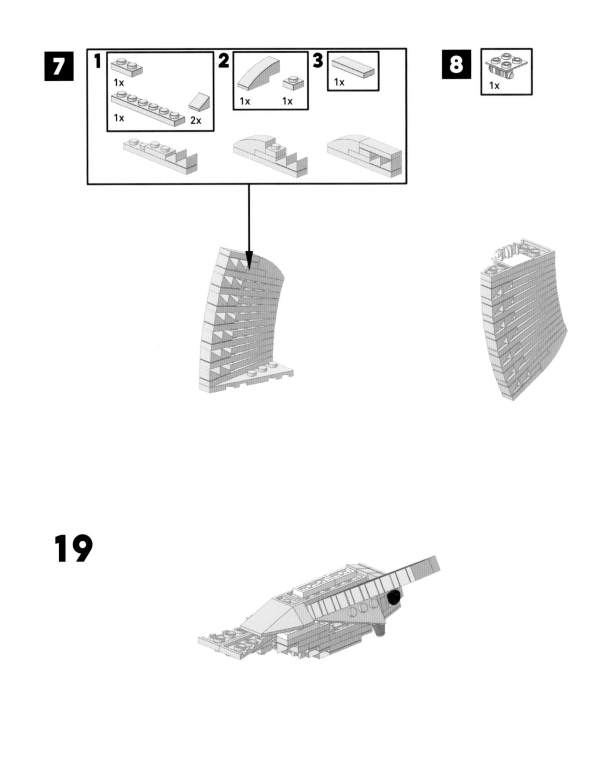

19

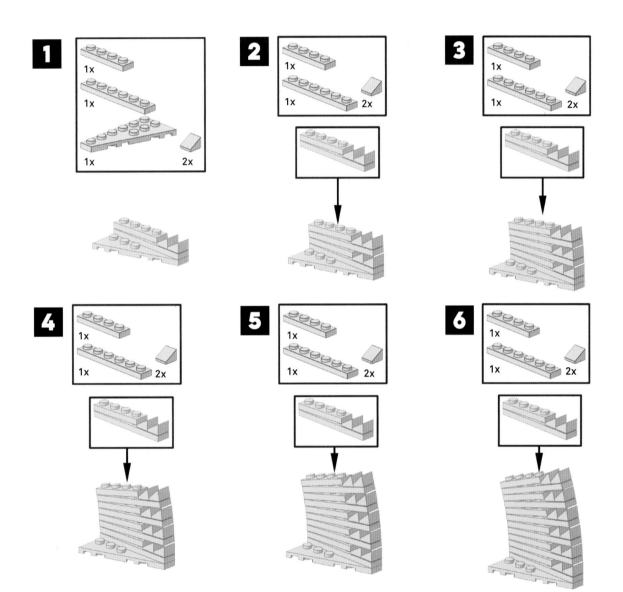

7

1 1x 1x 2x

2 1x 1x

3 1x

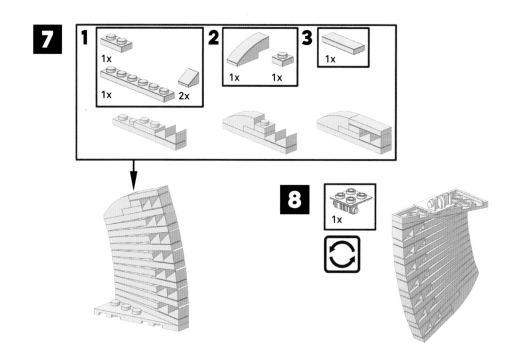

8 1x

20

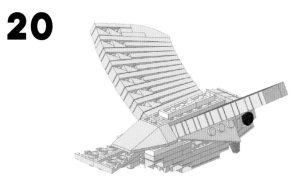

21 2x

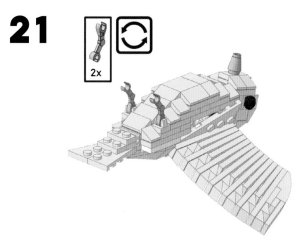

22

NORTHERN LAPWING

Vanellus vanellus

The northern lapwing (*Vanellus vanellus*) is native to Europe. It is affectionately known as the peewit, in imitation of its display calls. Its distinctive shape and coloring and its splendid crest attracted me to build it in LEGO.

- The northern lapwing is a medium-sized bird about 12 to 16 inches (30 to 40 cm) in length and belongs to the family *Charadriidae*.

- It can be seen all year round in the U.K.—in marshes, meadows, and moors and can be seen flocking on ploughed fields. They nest on the ground.

- It used to be a very common bird but has suffered significant decline in the past 25 years and has been placed on the highest conservation list (the Red List).

- Males and females are very similar. The female has a shorter crest and slightly less distinctive markings.

Parts Color Key

⬛	Black
⬛	Dark Bluish Gray
⬛	Dark Green
⬛	Dark Orange
⬛	Dark Purple
⬜	Light Bluish Gray
⬜	Light Pink
⬛	Red
☐	White

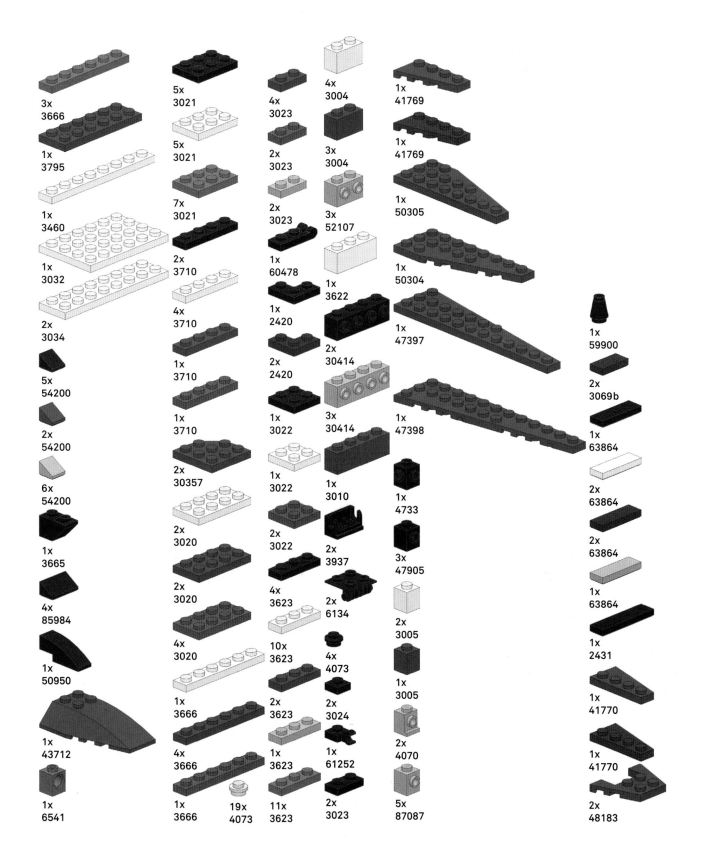

3x
3666

1x
3795

1x
3460

1x
3032

2x
3034

5x
54200

2x
54200

6x
54200

1x
3665

4x
85984

1x
50950

1x
43712

1x
6541

5x
3021

5x
3021

7x
3021

2x
3710

4x
3710

1x
3710

1x
3710

2x
30357

2x
3020

2x
3020

4x
3020

1x
3666

4x
3666

1x
3666

19x
4073

4x
3023

2x
3023

2x
3023

1x
60478

1x
2420

2x
2420

1x
3022

1x
3022

2x
3022

4x
3623

10x
3623

2x
3623

1x
3623

11x
3623

4x
3004

3x
3004

3x
52107

1x
3622

2x
30414

3x
30414

1x
3010

2x
3937

4x
4073

2x
3024

1x
61252

1x
41769

1x
41769

1x
50305

1x
50304

1x
47397

1x
47398

1x
4733

3x
47905

2x
6134

2x
3005

1x
3005

2x
4070

5x
87087

1x
59900

2x
3069b

1x
63864

2x
63864

2x
63864

1x
63864

1x
2431

1x
41770

1x
41770

2x
48183

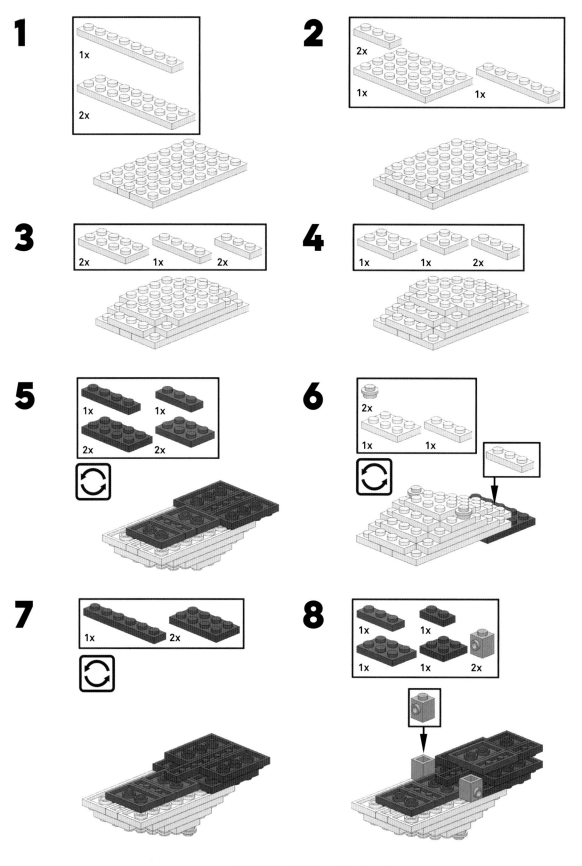

9

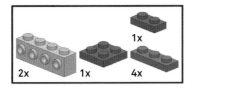

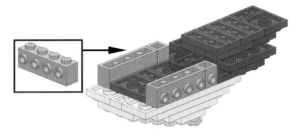

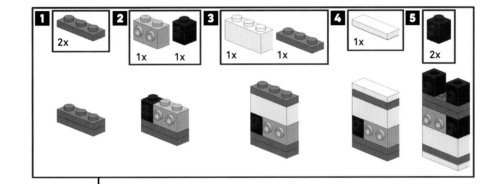

10

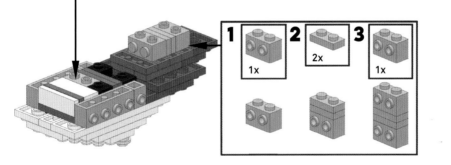

1 3x 1x

2 3x

3 1x 1x 2x

4 2x

5 1x 1x

6 1x 1x

7 1x

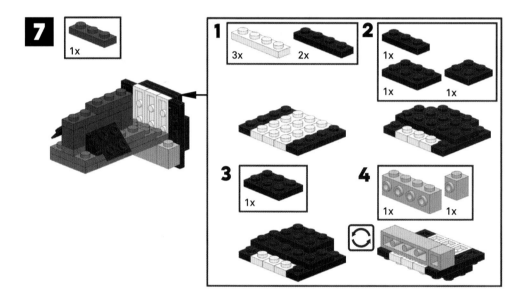

1 3x 2x

2 1x 1x 1x

3 1x

4 1x 1x

11

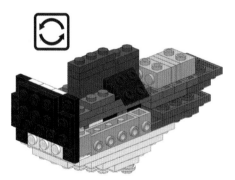

12

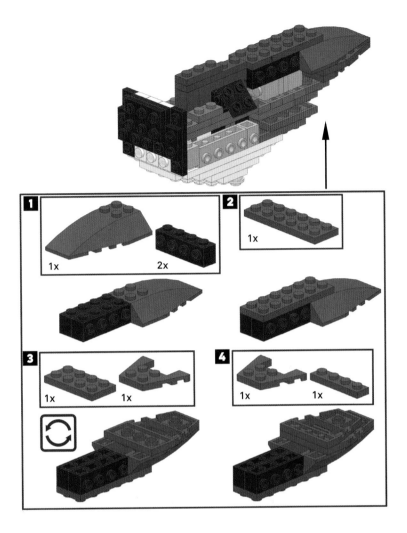

13

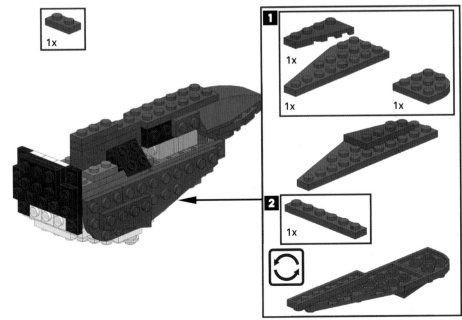

14

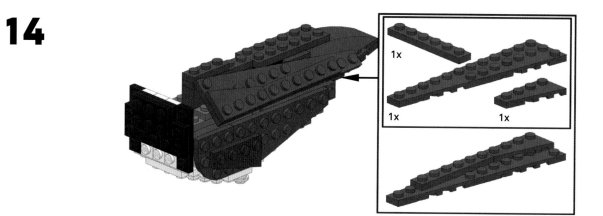

15

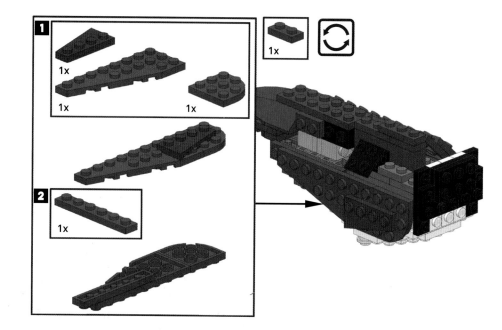

16

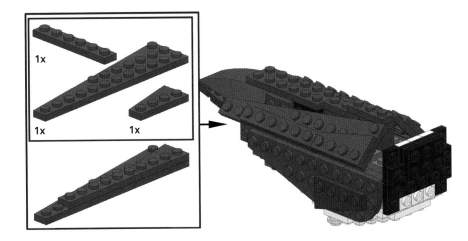

1 1x 1x

2 3x 2x

3 1x 2x 1x 2x

4 1x 1x

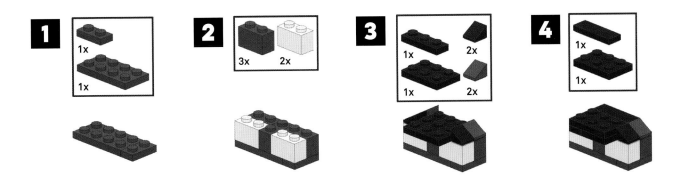

5 1x

6 1x 1x

7 1x 1x

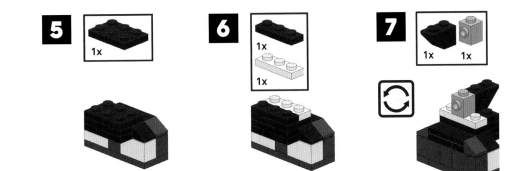

8

2x

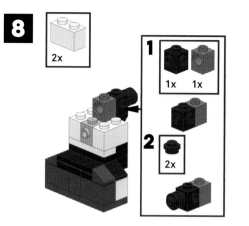

1
1x 1x

2
2x

9

1x 1x

10

2x 1x

11

1x 1x

12

1x 2x

13

2x 1x

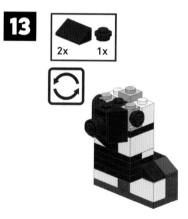

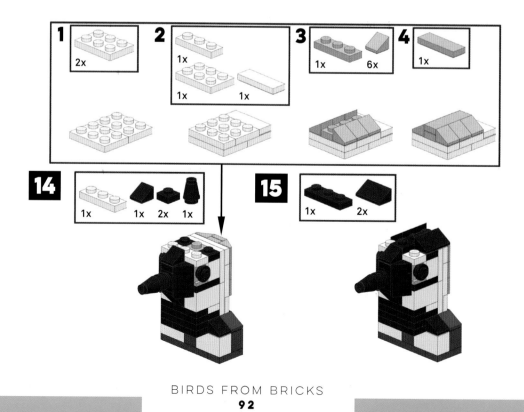

1
2x

2
1x 1x

3
1x 6x

4
1x

14
1x 1x 2x 1x

15
1x 2x

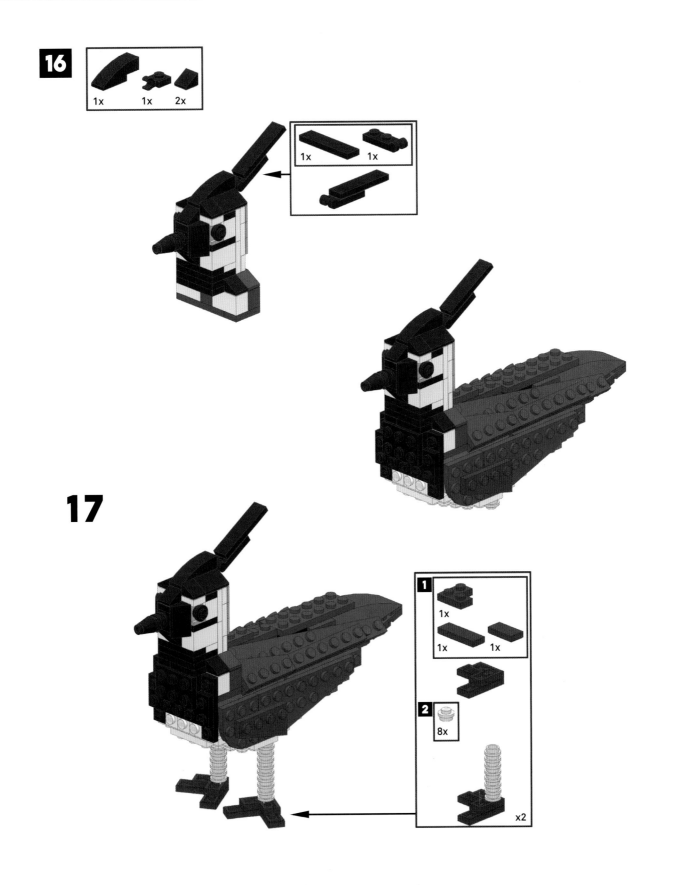

COMMON KINGFISHER
Alcedo Attis

The common kingfisher (*Alcedo Attis*), also known as the Eurasian kingfisher, is one of my favorite birds. It's one of the most colorful birds found in the U.K.

- Kingfishers are very territorial and frequently fight for their territory. They eat around 60 percent of their body weight a day and need a long stretch, around 0.6 miles (1 km), of riverbank.

- They are known as shy birds and are difficult to photograph as they fly fast and low over the water.

- At 6.3 inches (16 cm) long, they are not particularly large birds.

- They nest in riverbanks, with the male and female both helping to make the burrow.

Parts Color Key

- Black
- Blue
- Dark Azure
- Dark Bluish Gray
- Dark Orange
- Light Bluish Gray
- Medium Azure
- Medium Blue
- Orange
- Red
- Reddish Brown
- Tan
- Trans-Light Blue
- White

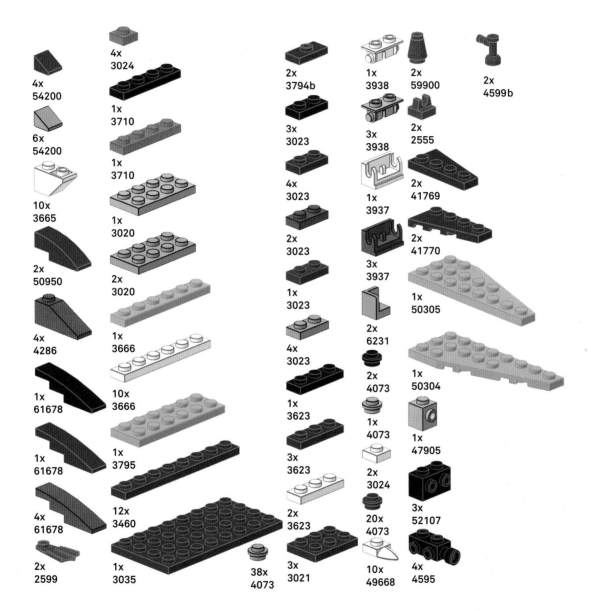

4x
54200

6x
54200

10x
3665

2x
50950

4x
4286

1x
61678

1x
61678

4x
61678

2x
2599

4x
3024

1x
3710

1x
3710

1x
3020

2x
3020

1x
3666

10x
3666

1x
3795

12x
3460

1x
3035

38x
4073

2x
3794b

3x
3023

4x
3023

2x
3023

1x
3023

4x
3023

1x
3623

3x
3623

2x
3623

3x
3021

1x
3938

3x
3938

1x
3937

3x
3937

2x
6231

2x
4073

1x
4073

20x
4073

10x
49668

2x
59900

2x
2555

2x
41769

2x
41770

1x
50305

1x
50304

1x
47905

3x
52107

4x
4595

2x
4599b

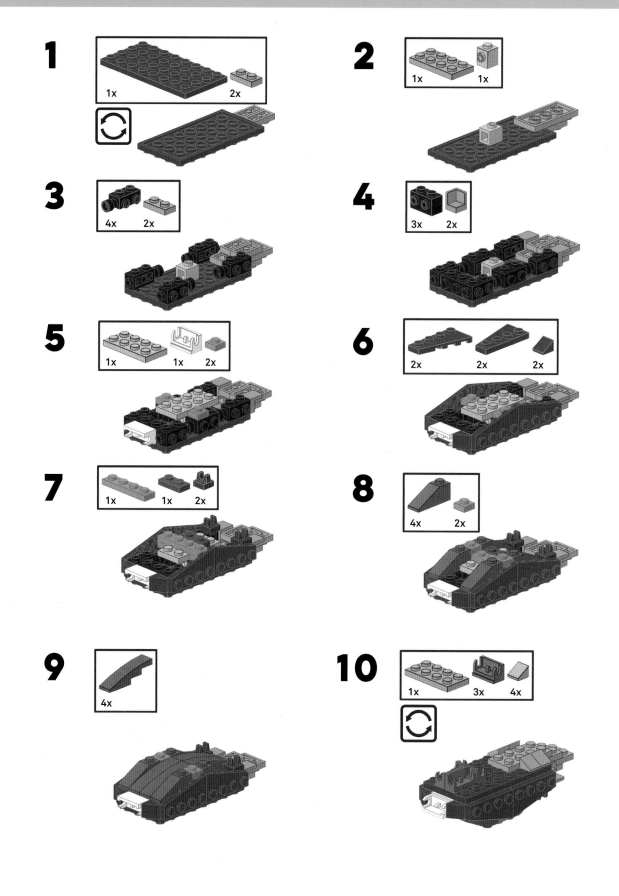

11

1 2x / 1x
2 2x
3 1x
4 1x

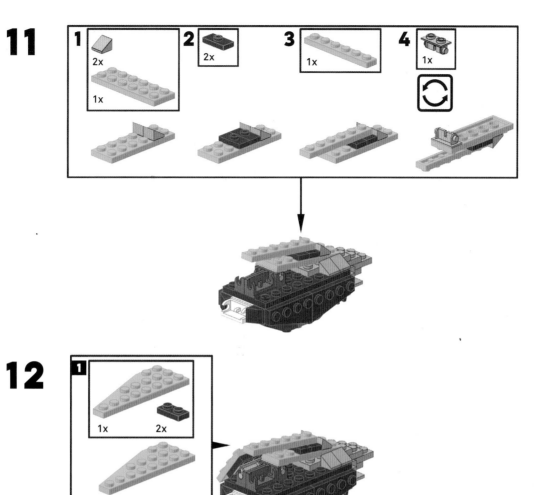

12

1 1x 2x
2 1x

13

1 2x / 1x
2 1x

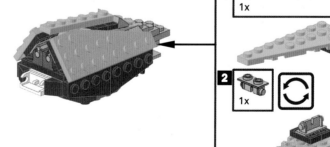

14

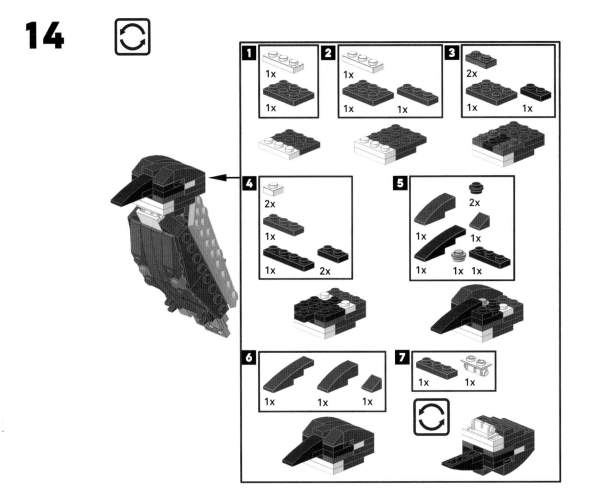

15

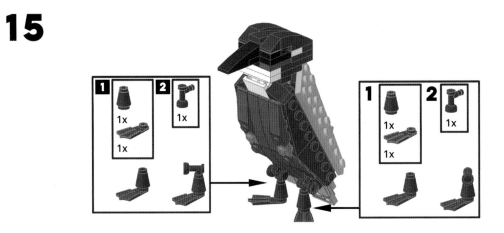

16

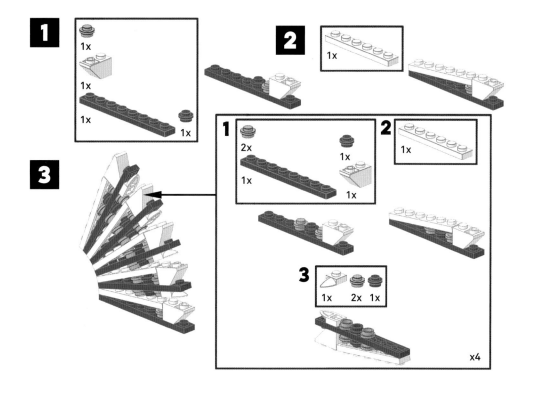

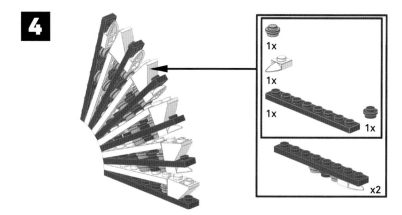

NORTH PACIFIC ALBATROSS

Phoebastria

The North Pacific albatross (*Phoebastria*) has the largest wingspan of any of the birds I have built so far. It was great fun to build and I would one day like to build one life-size and have it flying around in a museum.

- As their name suggests they are sea birds. They have the longest wingspan of any bird, up to 11.5 feet (3.5 m) in the wandering albatross.

- They can soar for thousands of miles without setting foot on land.

- When roosting, they choose isolated sites and lay one egg, with both parents incubating and raising the chick. They don't start breeding until they are at least 5 years old, sometimes up to a decade later. They mate for life and can live up to 60 years.

- They are classed as endangered, the main threat to life being fish bait on long line fishing. The birds dive for the bait before it sinks and get entangled on the hook and drown.

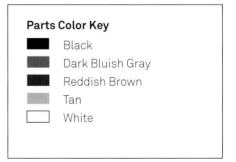

Parts Color Key

■	Black
■	Dark Bluish Gray
■	Reddish Brown
■	Tan
□	White

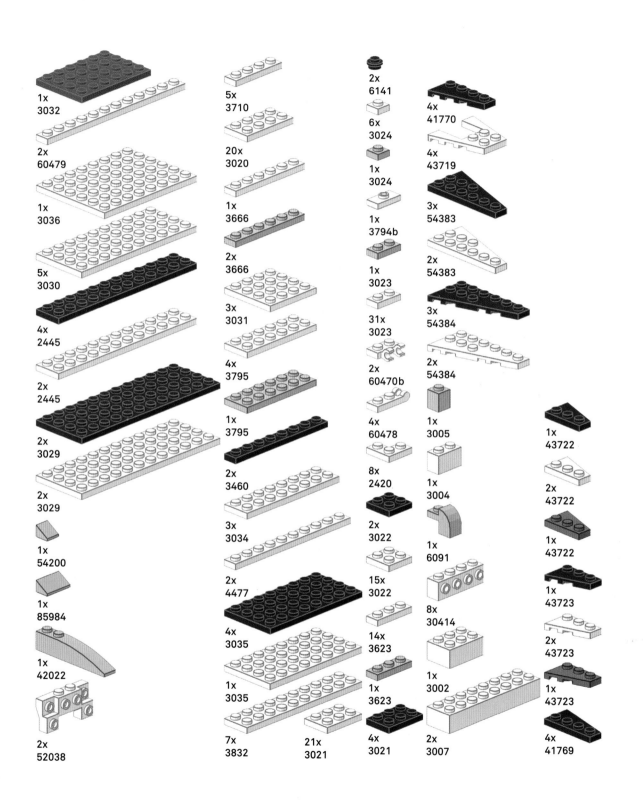

1x
3032

2x
60479

1x
3036

5x
3030

4x
2445

2x
2445

2x
3029

2x
3029

1x
54200

1x
85984

1x
42022

2x
52038

5x
3710

20x
3020

1x
3666

2x
3666

3x
3031

4x
3795

1x
3795

2x
3460

3x
3034

2x
4477

4x
3035

1x
3035

7x
3832

21x
3021

2x
6141

6x
3024

1x
3024

1x
3794b

1x
3023

31x
3023

2x
60470b

4x
60478

8x
2420

2x
3022

15x
3022

14x
3623

1x
3623

4x
3021

4x
41770

4x
43719

3x
54383

2x
54383

3x
54384

2x
54384

1x
3005

1x
3004

1x
6091

8x
30414

1x
3002

2x
3007

1x
43722

2x
43722

1x
43722

1x
43723

2x
43723

1x
43723

4x
41769

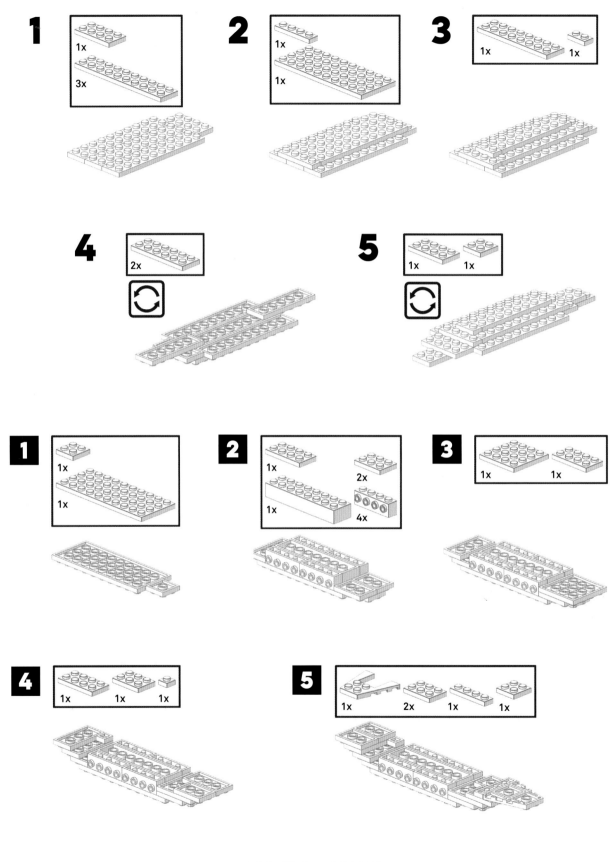

6

1x 2x 1x 2x

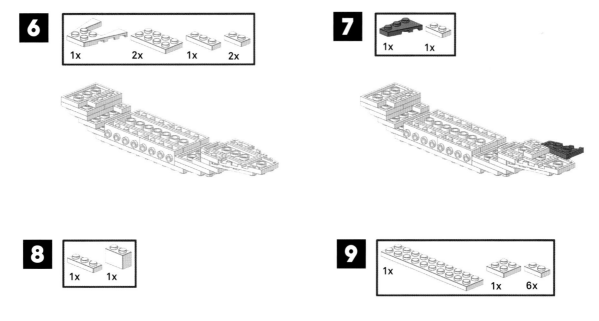

7

1x 1x

8

1x 1x

9

1x 1x 6x

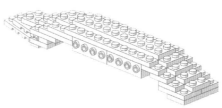

6

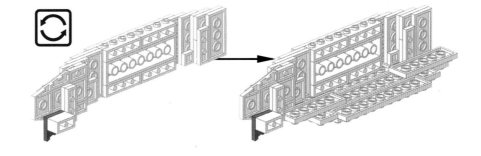

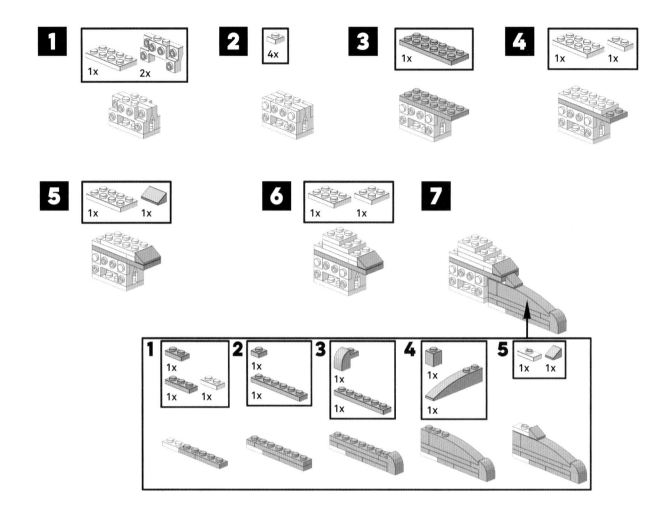

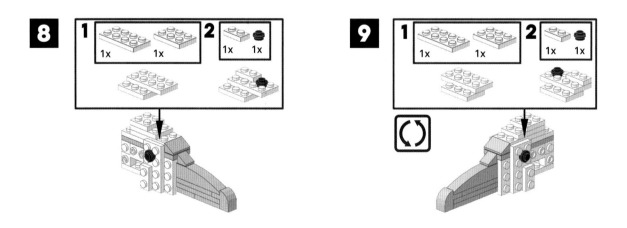

7

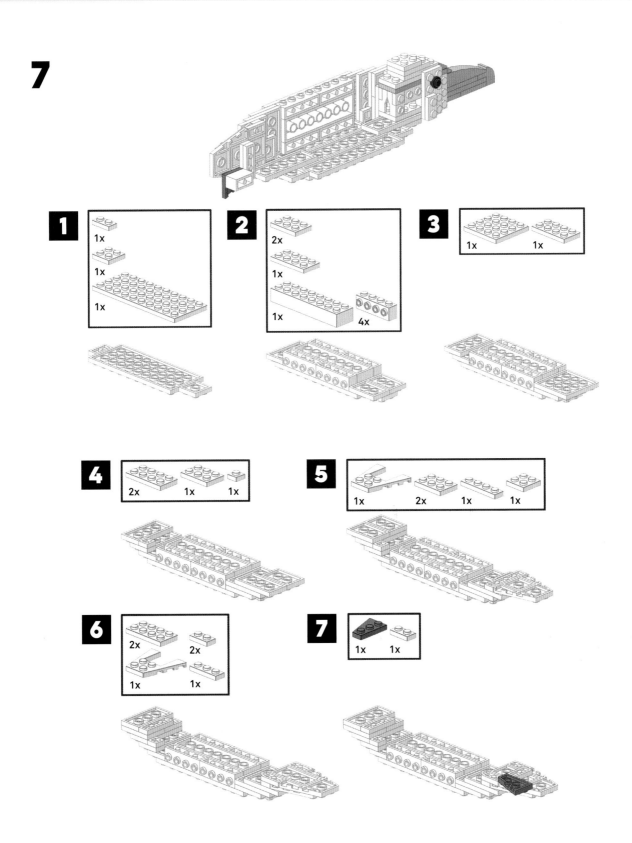

8

1x 1x

9

1x 1x 5x

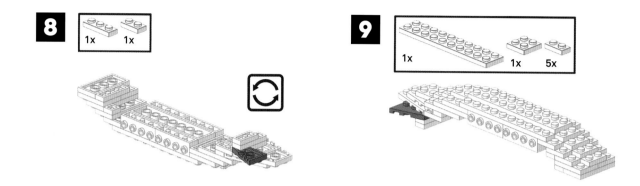

8

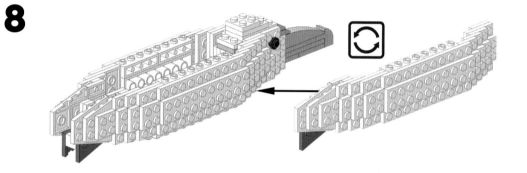

9

1		2		3	
2x	1x	1x		2x	1x
		1x	1x		

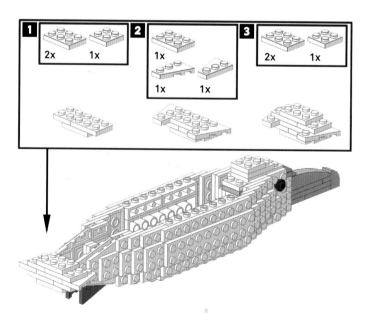

1

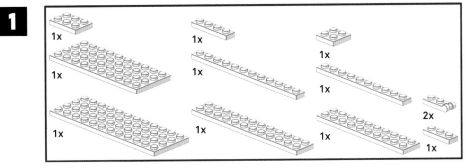

1x 1x 1x 1x 1x 1x 1x 1x 1x 2x 1x

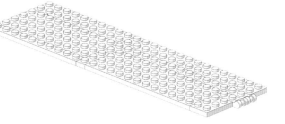

2

2x 2x 1x 1x 2x 2x

10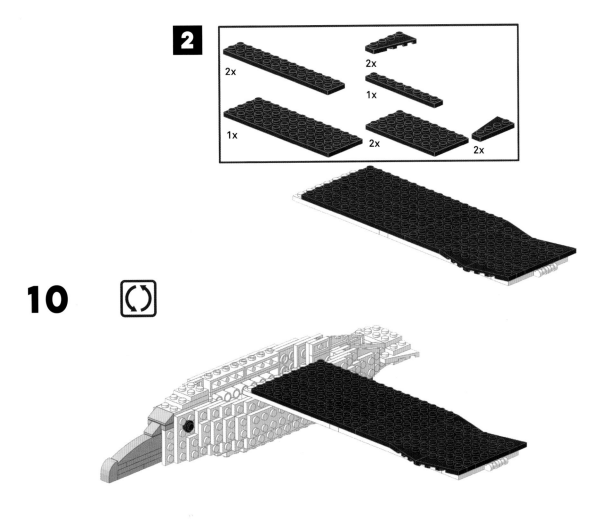

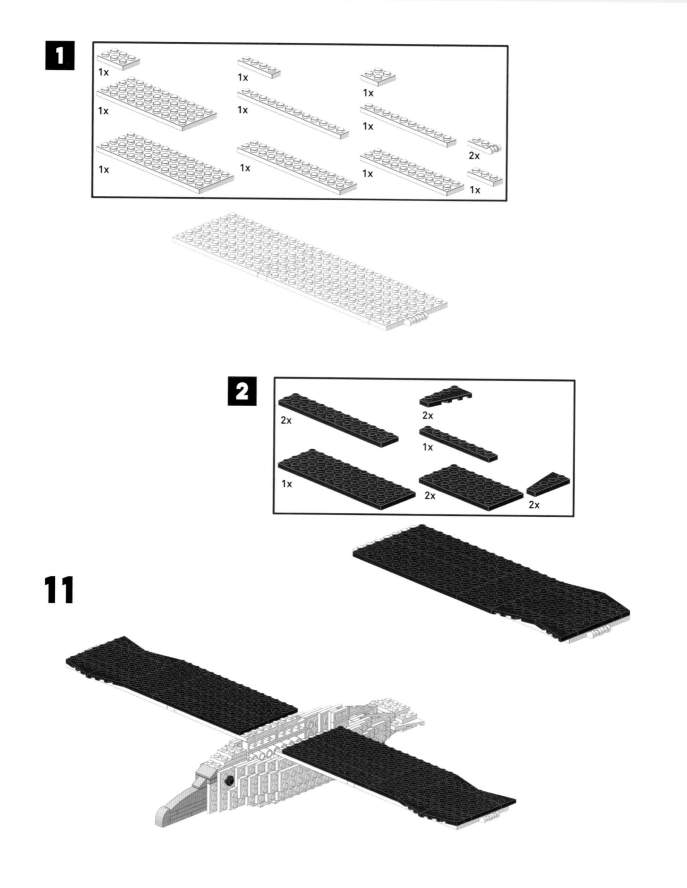

11

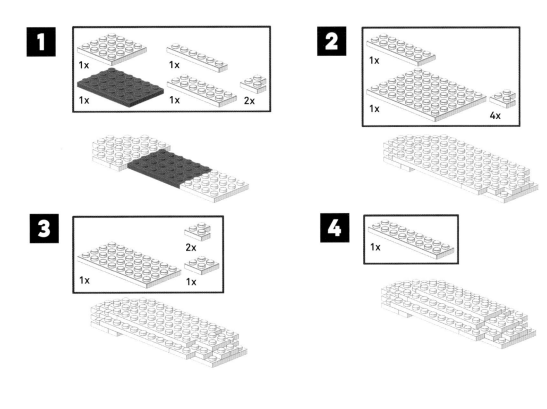

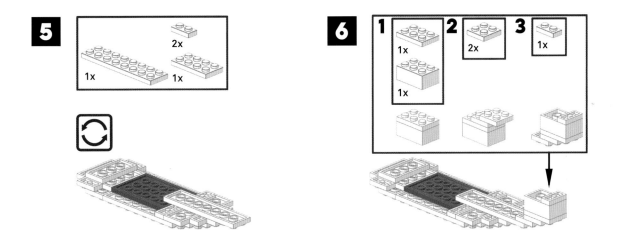

12

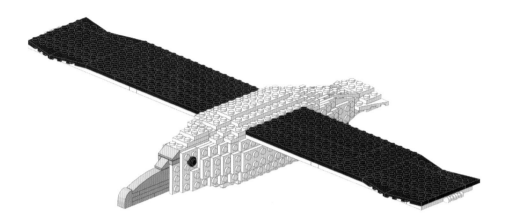

1

1x

2x 2x 1x 1x

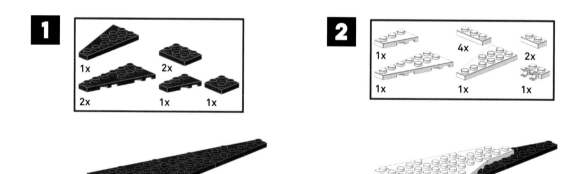

2

1x 4x 2x

1x 1x 1x

13

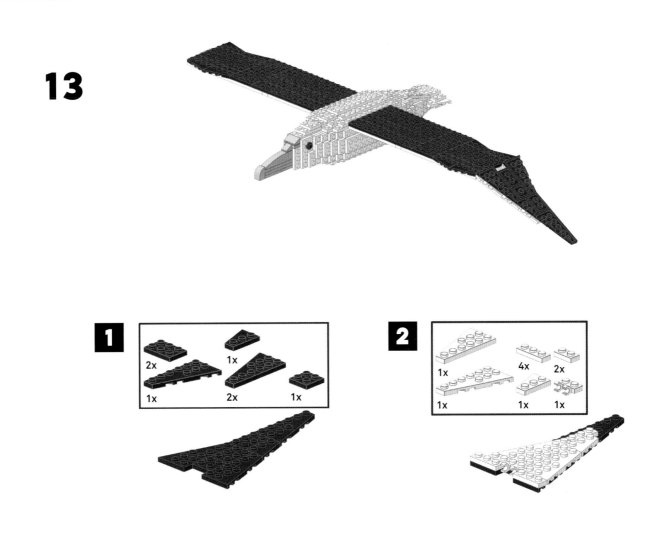

1
2x 1x
1x 2x 1x

2
1x 4x 2x
1x 1x 1x

14

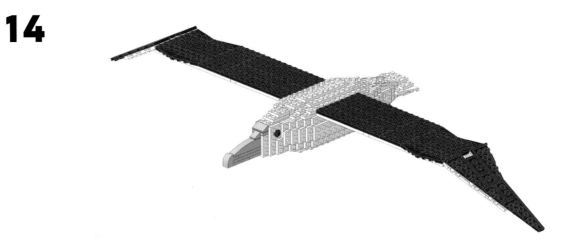

PINK ROBIN

Petroica rodinogaster

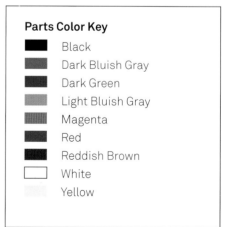

I built the pink robin (*Petroica rodinogaster*) as part of my Australasian collection. The breast feathers really are a vivid shade of pink in the male bird. The female is quite dowdy by comparison, being mainly grayish brown in color.

- The pink robin is not closely related to the European nor the American robin.

- It can be found in the forests in the southern states of Australia and in Tasmania.

- Pink robins eat mainly spiders and insects, including caterpillars, beetles, wasps, flies, and ants.

Parts Color Key

- Black
- Dark Bluish Gray
- Dark Green
- Light Bluish Gray
- Magenta
- Red
- Reddish Brown
- White
- Yellow

For instructions on building the perch, see page 138.

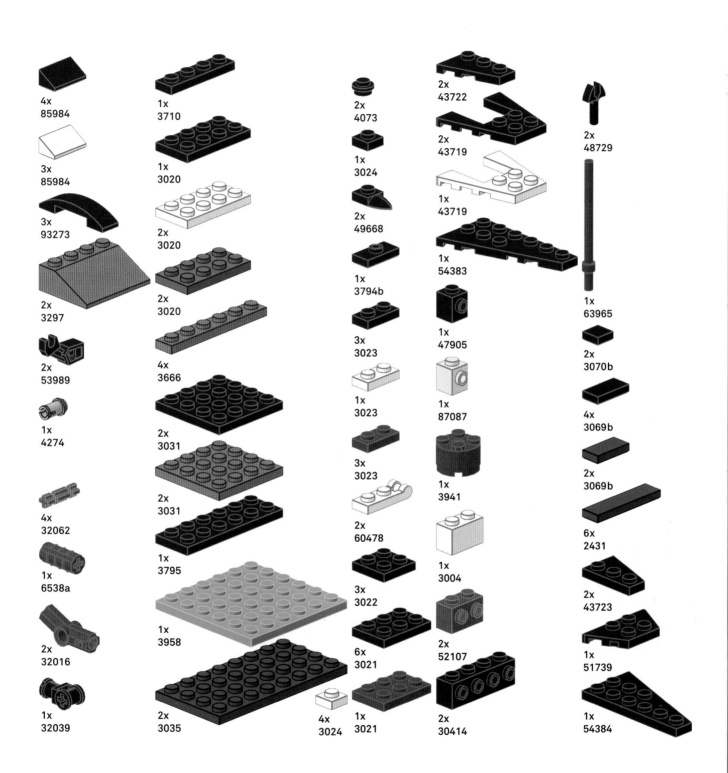

4x
85984

3x
85984

3x
93273

2x
3297

2x
53989

1x
4274

4x
32062

1x
6538a

2x
32016

1x
32039

1x
3710

1x
3020

2x
3020

2x
3020

4x
3666

2x
3031

2x
3031

1x
3795

1x
3958

2x
3035

2x
4073

1x
3024

2x
49668

1x
3794b

3x
3023

1x
3023

3x
3023

2x
60478

3x
3022

6x
3021

4x
3024

1x
3021

2x
43722

2x
43719

1x
43719

1x
54383

1x
47905

1x
87087

1x
3941

1x
3004

2x
52107

2x
30414

2x
48729

1x
63965

2x
3070b

4x
3069b

2x
3069b

6x
2431

2x
43723

1x
51739

1x
54384

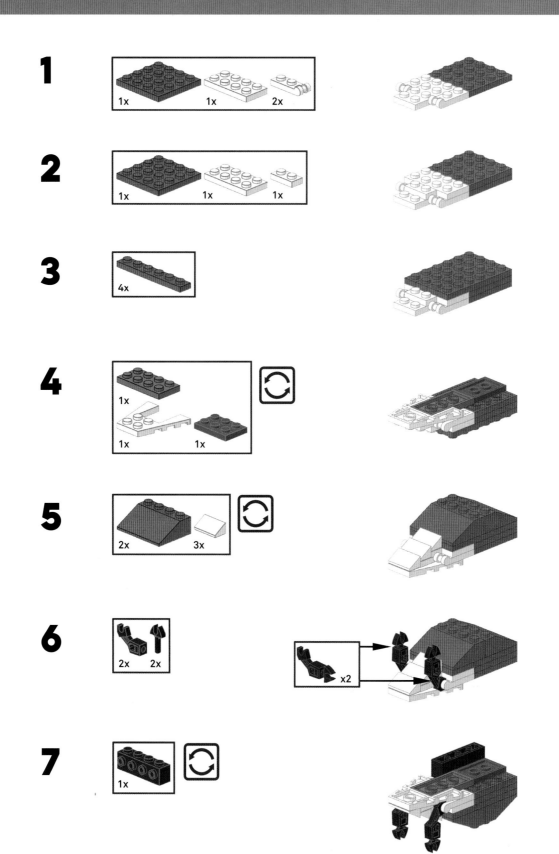

1 1x 1x 2x

2 1x 1x 1x

3 4x

4 1x 1x 1x

5 2x 3x

6 2x 2x x2

7 1x

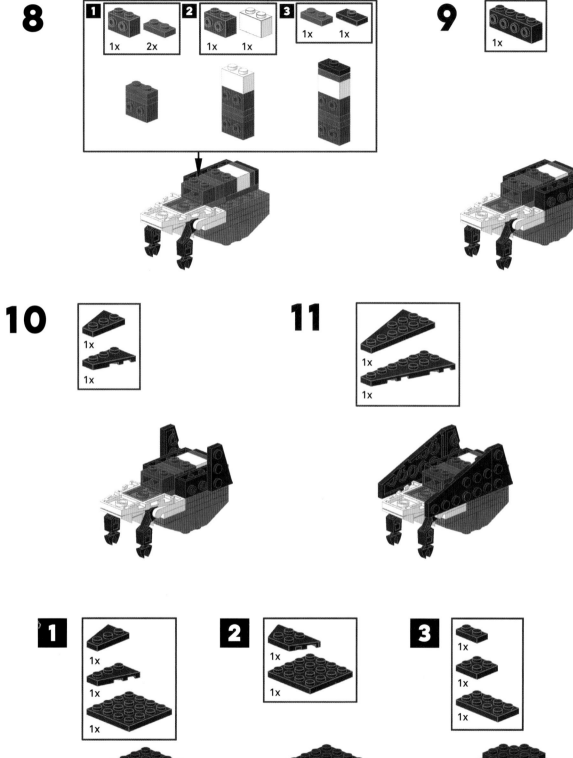

4 1x

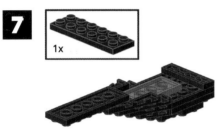

5 1x 1x 1x

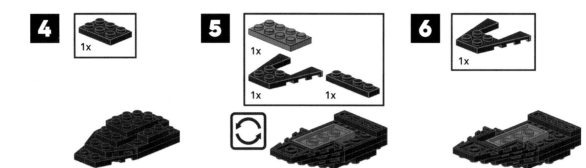

6 1x

7 1x

12

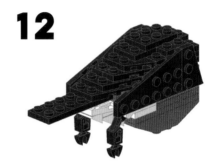

1 1x 1x 1x

2 1x

3 3x

4 1x 1x 1x

5 1x 2x

6

1 1x **2** 1x 1x

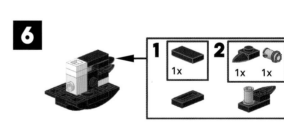

7

1
1x
1x

2
1x
1x 1x 1x

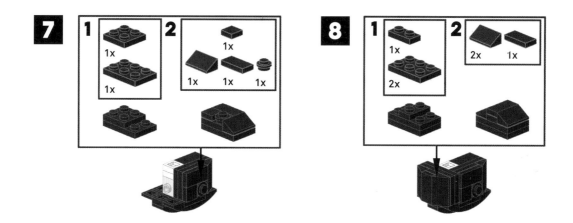

8

1
1x
2x

2
2x 1x

9

1
1x
1x

2
1x
1x
1x 1x

13

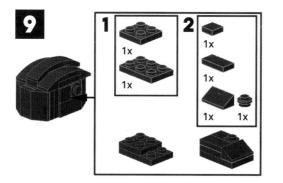

KAKAPO
Strigops habroptilus

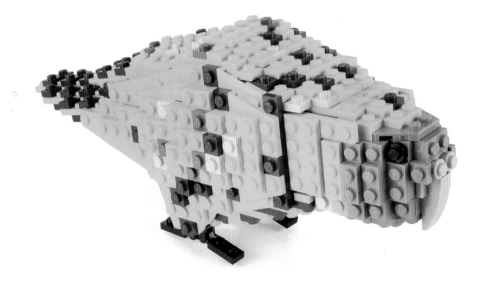

The kakapo (*Strigops habroptilus*) is an extraordinary looking bird! I just had to build it in LEGO as part of my Australasia / Oceania collection.

- The kakapo is native to New Zealand and is the world's rarest, heaviest, and strangest flightless parrot.

- For hundreds of years it had no predators, so it had no need of flight. Because of Polynesian and European colonization and the introduction of cats, rats, ferrets, and stoats, the kakapo was almost wiped out.

- It is critically endangered with less than 130 known birds in existence today. Kakapos are now kept on three predator-free islands.

Parts Color Key

- ■ Black
- ■ Dark Bluish Gray
- ■ Dark Tan
- ■ Light Bluish Gray
- ■ Lime
- ■ Red
- ■ Reddish Brown
- ■ Tan
- □ White

2x
2420

20x
3666

4x
3666

1x
3031

1x
3031

11x
3031

8x
3795

1x
3795

2x
3460

1x
3032

1x
3958

1x
50950

1x
99207

14x
3022

2x
2450

2x
3021

3x
3021

2x
3021

2x
3710

26x
3710

2x
3710

4x
3710

4x
3020

1x
3020

23x
3020

1x
3666

9x
3024

19x
3023

2x
3023

2x
63868

6x
63868

2x
60478

6x
60478

1x
2420

1x
2420

26x
2420

12x
2420

2x
87580

9x
3022

1x
3623

21x
3623

2x
3623

2x
87087

4x
44301

4x
44302

2x
4073

2x
4073

5x
3024

1x
3024

17x
3024

48x
3024

4x
3794b

1x
3794b

1x
3794b

5x
3023

47x
3023

12x
3023

2x
41769

4x
87087

2x
11211

2x
3004

1x
3004

1x
3003

1x
3003

6x
30414

5x
3001

1x
3009

4x
2456

11x
43723

1x
51739

12x
43722

3x
41770

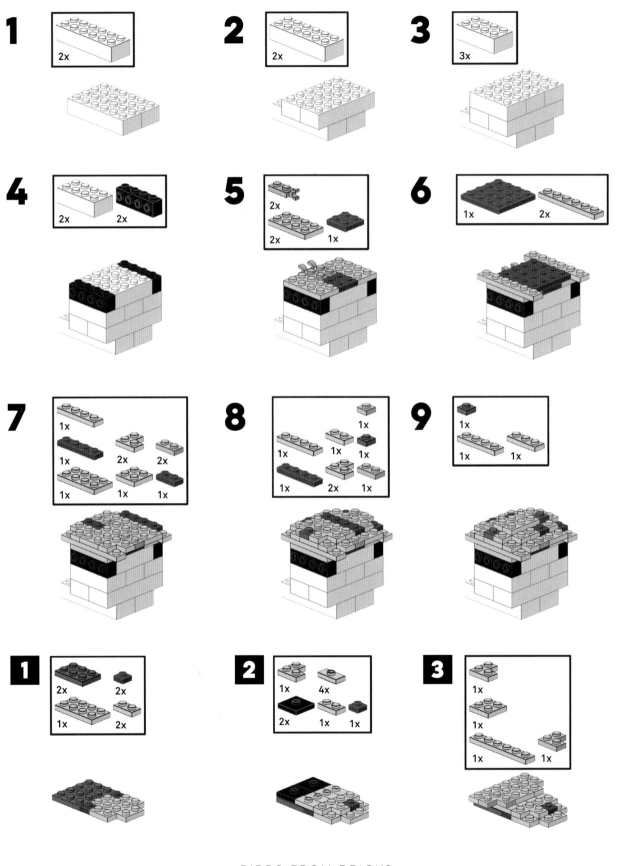

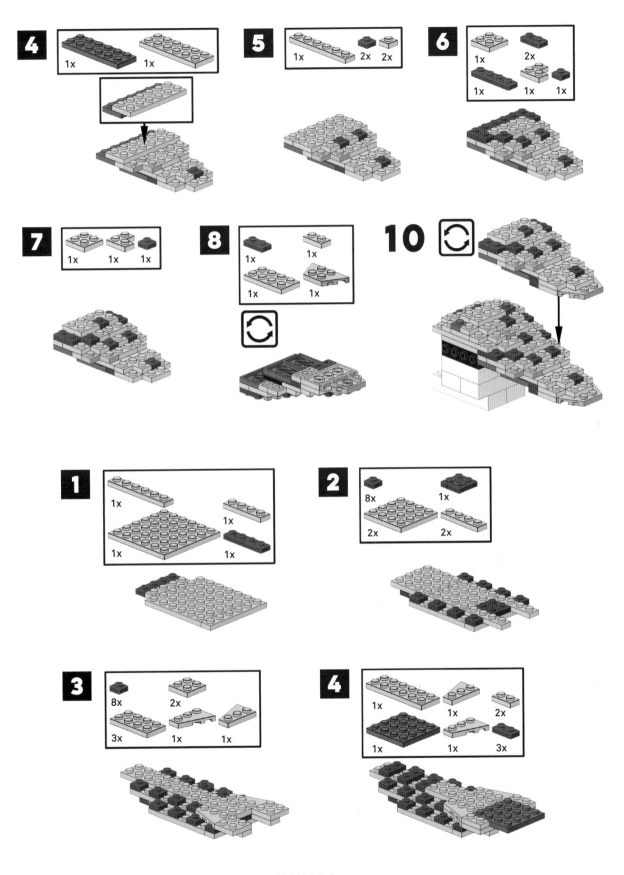

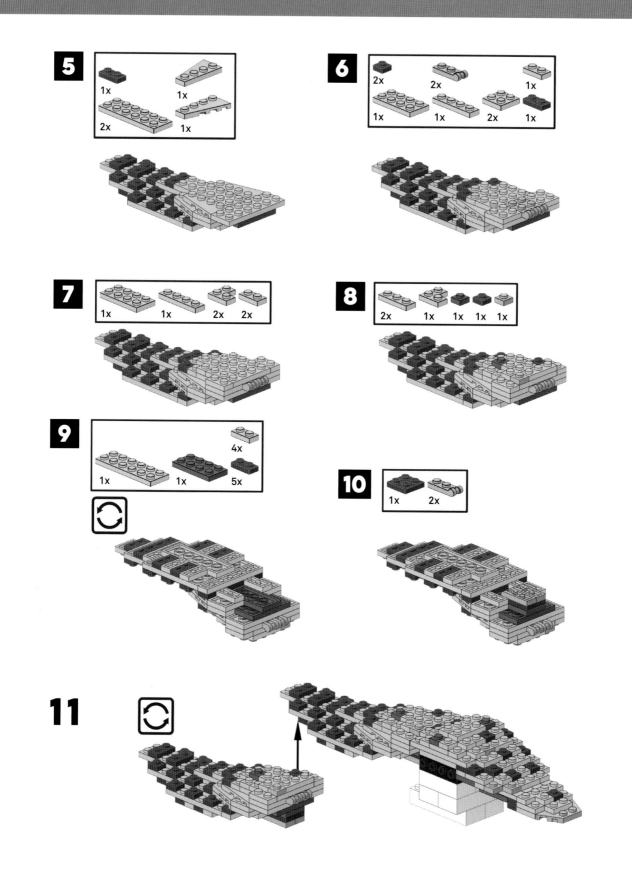

1

1x
1x 1x

2 2x

3 1x 1x

4 1x
1x 1x

5 1x 1x

6 2x
1x 4x

7 1x
1x 1x

8 1x 1x

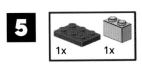

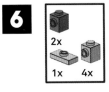

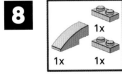

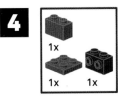

9 1x 2x

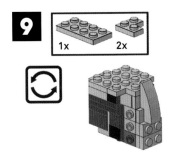

10 2x

11

1 1x
1x 3x

2 1x 1x
1x 2x

3 3x
1x 2x

4 1x 1x
1x 1x 1x

5 1x 1x

2x

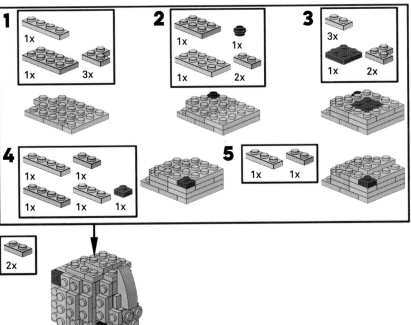

12

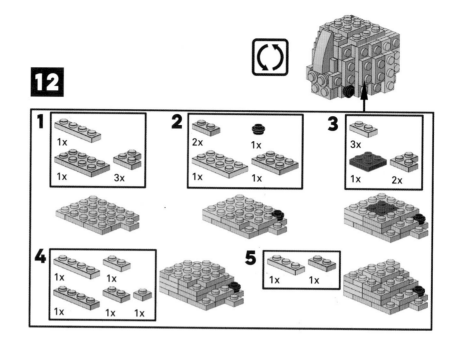

1
1x
1x 3x

2
2x 1x
1x 1x

3
3x
1x 2x

4
1x 1x
1x 1x 1x

5
1x 1x

12

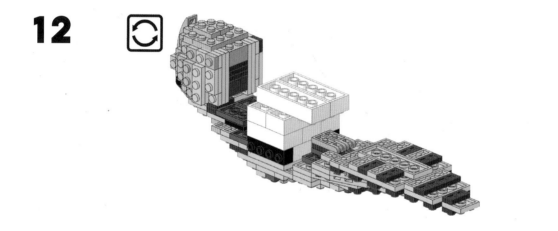

1

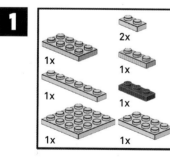

2x
1x
1x
1x 1x
1x 1x

2

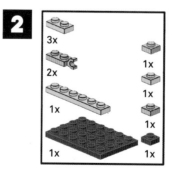

3x
2x
1x
1x
1x
1x
1x
1x

3

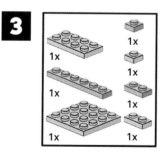

1x
1x
1x
1x
1x
1x
1x

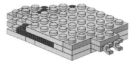

4

1x
1x
1x
1x
1x

5

1x
1x
2x

6

2x
1x
3x

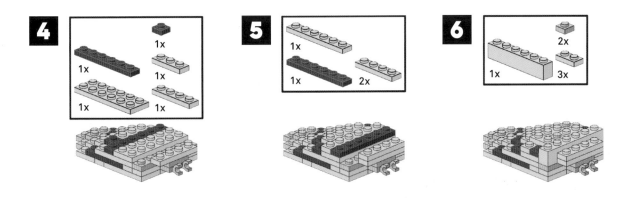

7

1x
2x
1x
1x
1x

8

1x
1x

9

1x
2x

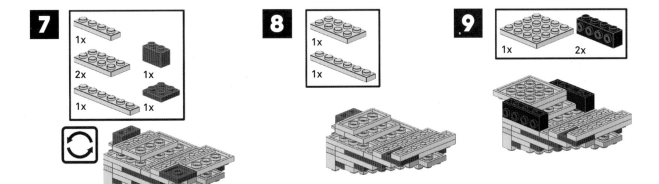

13

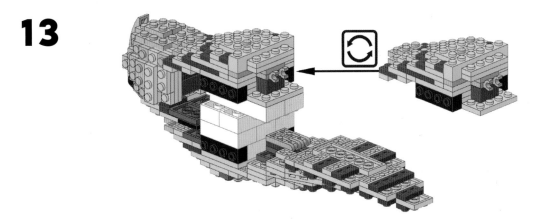

14

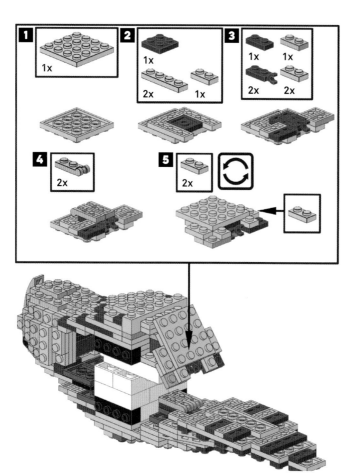

15

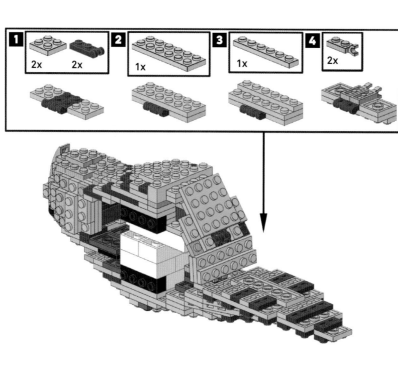

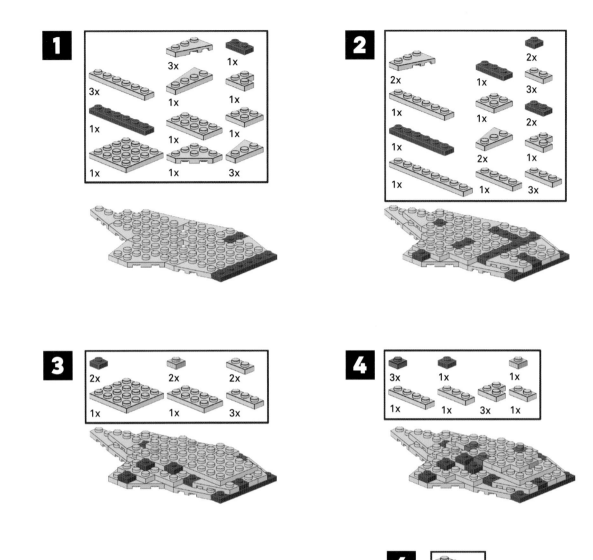

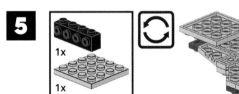

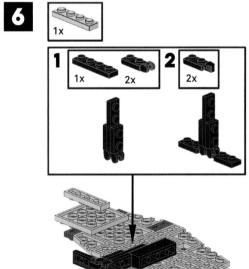

4x 1x 3x 2x

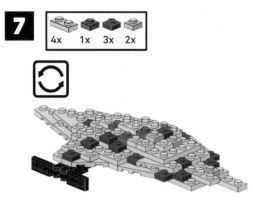

16

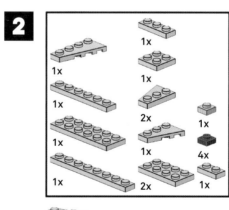

1x   3x   1x

1x   3x   1x

4x   1x   1x

1x   1x   1x

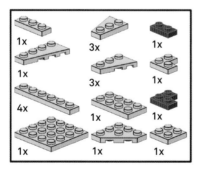

2

1x

1x   1x

1x   2x   1x

1x   1x   4x

1x   2x   1x

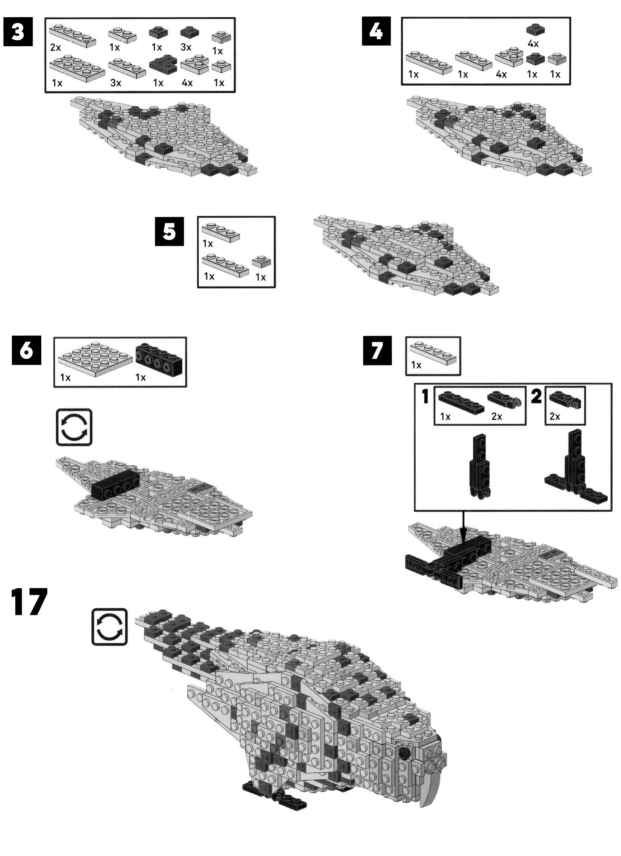

SULPHUR-CRESTED COCKATOO

Cacatua galerita

The sulphur-crested cockatoo (*Cacatua galerita*) has a look of mischief about it and I had fun building it, especially its striking bright yellow crest.

- This cockatoo is found in wooded habitats in Australia, New Guinea, and part of Indonesia. They are also common in urban areas and can become a nuisance. They're very noisy, raucous birds, and tend to live in large flocks.

- Males and females have almost identical plumage. They both take turns in raising their young, which stay with their parents for a number of months.

- Their intelligence and quirky behavior make them popular as pets, living up to 70 years in captivity. They need lots of mental and physical stimulation. There's a ban on importing them to the U.S.

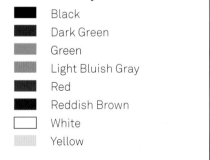

Parts Color Key

■	Black
■	Dark Green
■	Green
■	Light Bluish Gray
■	Red
■	Reddish Brown
□	White
■	Yellow

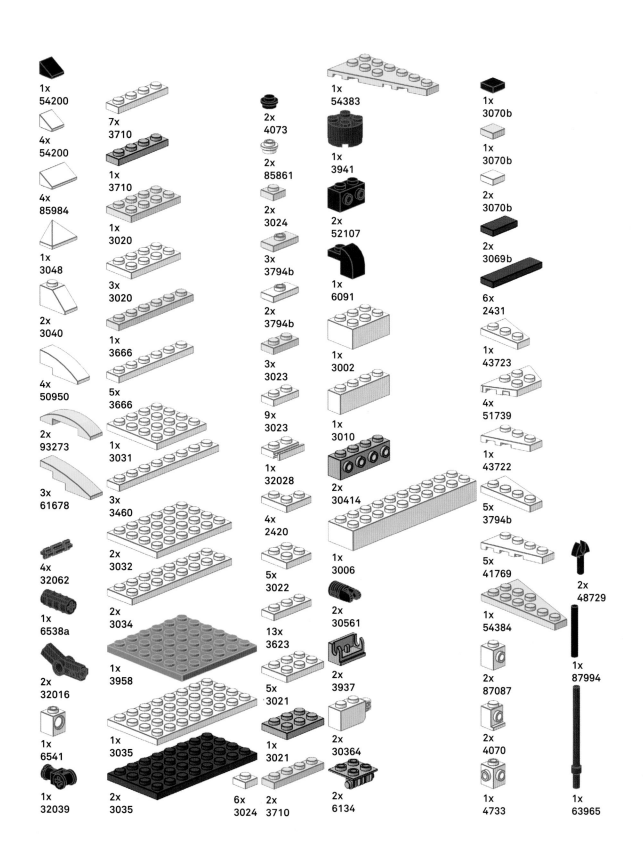

1x
54200

4x
54200

4x
85984

1x
3048

2x
3040

4x
50950

2x
93273

3x
61678

4x
32062

1x
6538a

2x
32016

1x
6541

1x
32039

7x
3710

1x
3710

1x
3020

3x
3020

1x
3666

5x
3666

1x
3031

3x
3460

2x
3032

2x
3034

1x
3958

1x
3035

2x
3035

2x
4073

2x
85861

2x
3024

3x
3794b

2x
3794b

3x
3023

9x
3023

1x
32028

4x
2420

5x
3022

13x
3623

5x
3021

1x
3021

6x
3024

1x
54383

1x
3941

2x
52107

1x
6091

1x
3002

1x
3010

2x
30414

1x
3006

2x
30561

2x
3937

2x
30364

2x
6134

2x
3710

1x
3070b

1x
3070b

2x
3070b

2x
3069b

6x
2431

1x
43723

4x
51739

1x
43722

5x
3794b

5x
41769

1x
54384

2x
87087

2x
4070

1x
4733

2x
48729

1x
87994

1x
63965

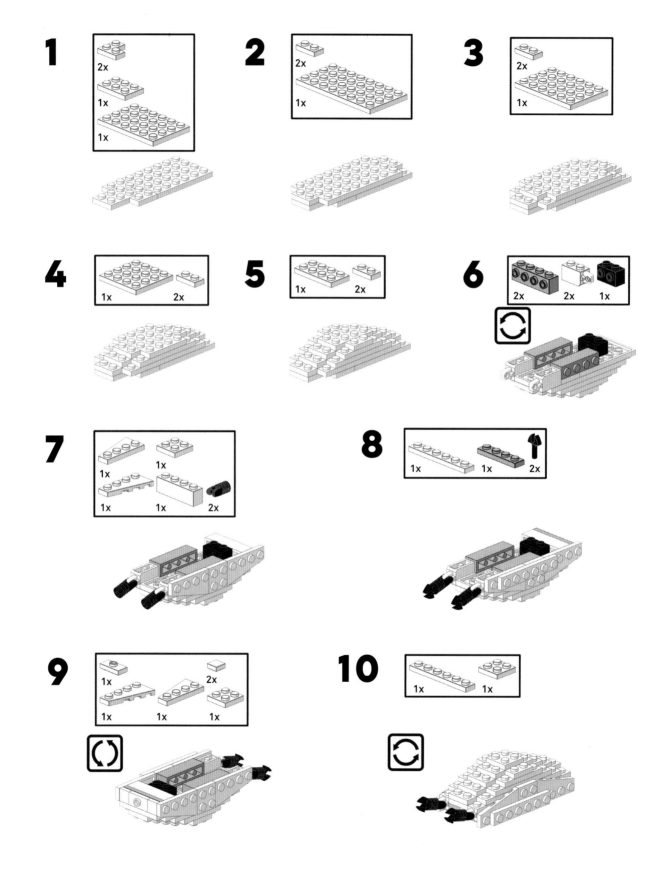

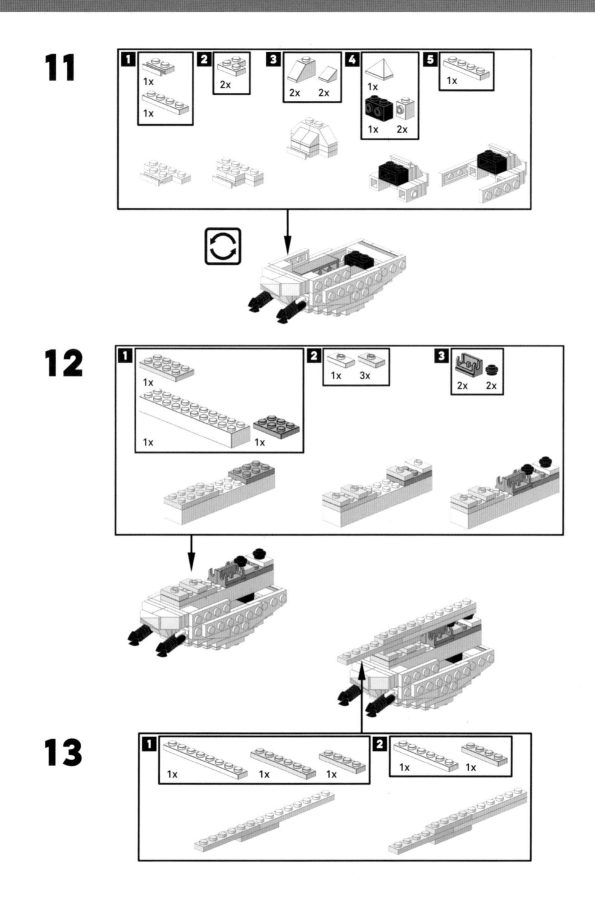

14

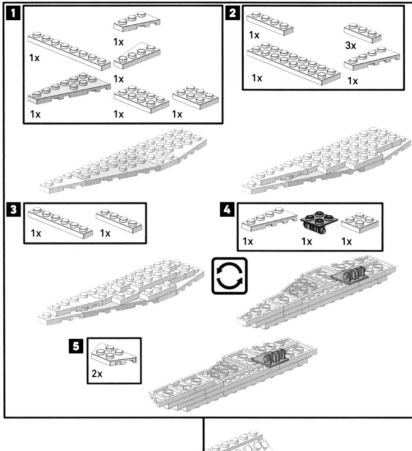

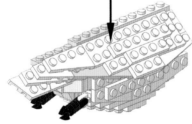

15

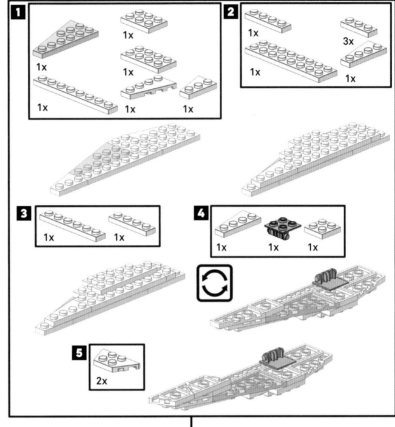

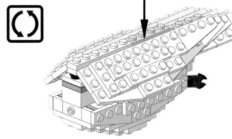

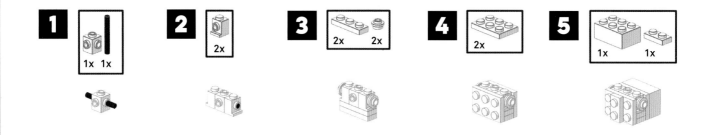

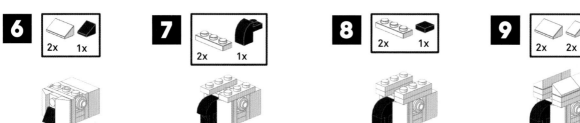

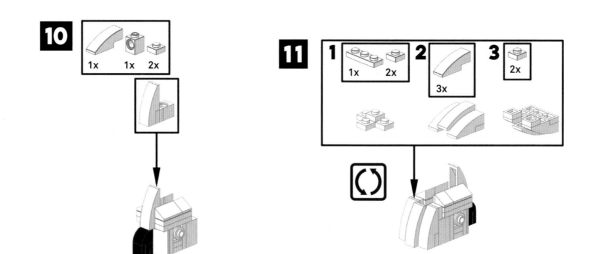

16

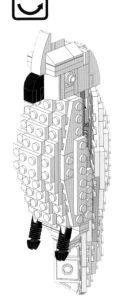

17

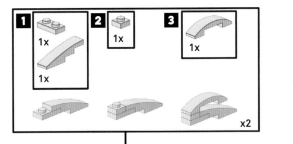

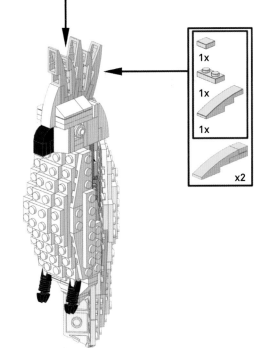

PERCH INSTRUCTIONS

The instructions below are to make the perch shown with the northern cardinal (page 6), the red-capped robin-chat (page 62), the canary (page 74), the pink robin (page 112), and the sulphur-crested cockatoo (page 130). The parts for the perch are included in the inventories for each of these bird models.

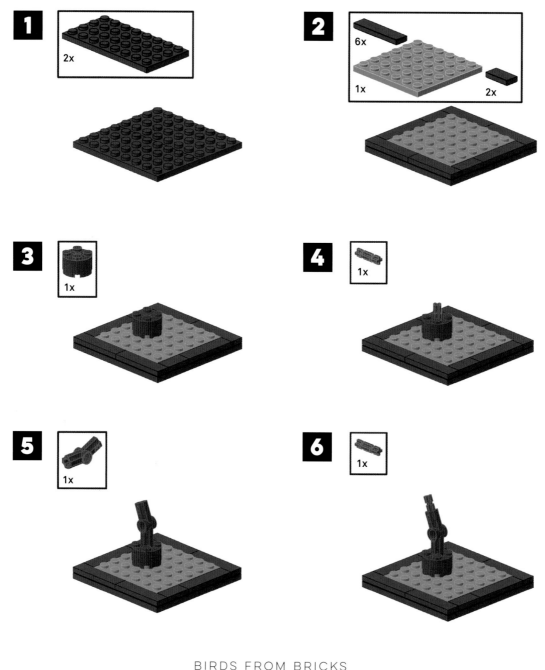

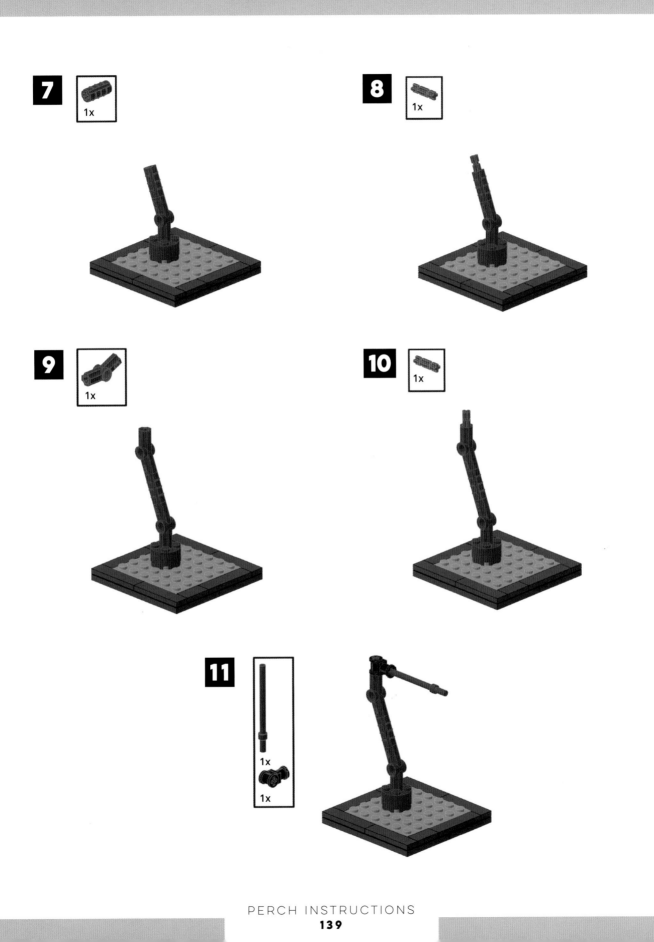

RESOURCES

Birds

African Bird Club
www.africanbirdclub.org

American Bird Conservancy
www.abcbirds.org

Avibase: The World Bird Database
avibase.bsc-eoc.org/avibase.jsp

BirdLife International
www.birdlife.org

BirdLife Australia
birdlife.org.au

Bird Studies Canada
www.birdscanada.org

Birdnet: The Ornithological Council
www.nmnh.si.edu/BIRDNET

Birds.com
www.birds.com

Birds of Europe
www.birdsofeurope.org

Birds of the World: An Online Bird Book
www.carolinabirds.org

Cornell Lab of Ornithology
www.allaboutbirds.org
www.birds.cornell.edu

Ecology Asia
www.ecologyasia.com/verts/birds.htm

Great Backyard Bird Count
gbbc.birdcount.org

The Institute for Bird Populations
www.birdpop.org

National Audubon Society
www.audubon.org

National Geographic
animals.nationalgeographic.com/animals/birds

Ornithology.com
www.ornithology.com

Royal Society for the Protection of Birds
www.rspb.org.uk

Bricks

BrickLink
www.bricklink.com

Brickmania
www.brickmania.com

Brickworld.us
www.brickworld.us

Brick Owl
www.brickowl.com

Bricks & Minifigs
www.bricksandminifigs.com

Brickset
www.brickset.com

LEGO
www.lego.com

GALLERY

Northern
Cardinal
page 6

Painted
Bunting
page 22

Canary
page 74

Red-Capped
Robin-Chat
page 62

Sulphur-
Crested
Cockatoo
page 130

Northern
Lapwing
page 84

Pink Robin
page 112

North Pacific
Albatross
page 100

Common
Grackle
page 14

Andean
Cock-of-
the-Rock
page 30

Northern
Rockhopper
Penguin
page 52

Common
Kingfisher
page 94

Kakapo
page 118

Scarlet
Macaw
page 30

Eurasian
Blue Tit
page 68

ABOUT THE AUTHOR

A passionate nature and bird lover and a former gardener and tree surgeon, professional LEGO builder **THOMAS POULSOM** rediscovered his love of building with LEGO as an adult. He was inspired to create his first realistic LEGO bird sculpture, a robin, when a real robin perched nearby while he worked in his garden. Poulsom has since expanded the scope of his LEGO bird project to more than 80 species of birds from every continent. Three of his designs—his robin, hummingbird, and blue jay—were produced by LEGO as an official set in 2015, and his other LEGO bird designs have been featured in many media outlets, including television, radio, and online venues for design, gardening, nature, and birding. In 2013 he was a speaker at the PINC (People Ideas Nature Creativity) Conference in Zeist, Holland. Poulsom now works on all types of LEGO commissions. He lives in Bristol, England.